W9-BNH-330

THE

5 IN *10*

COOKBOOK

THE
5 IN 10
COOKBOOK

5 Ingredients in

10 Minutes or Less

PAULA J. HAMILTON

A JOHN BOSWELL ASSOCIATES / KING HILL PRODUCTIONS BOOK

HEARST BOOKS

NEW YORK

This book is dedicated to
Edward, Julia and Jeffrey,
who make family dinners so important.

It is the policy of William Morrow and Company, Inc., and its imprints and affiliates recognizing the importance of preserving what has been written, to print the books we publish on acid-free paper, and we exert our best efforts to that end.

Library of Congress Cataloging-in-Publication Data
Hamilton, Paula J.
    The 5 in 10 cookbook : 5 ingredients in 10 minutes or less / Paula J. Hamilton.
        p.   cm.
    Includes index.
    ISBN 0-688-11927-1
    1. Quick amd easy cookery. I. Title. II. Title: Five in ten cookbook.
    TX833.5.H35   1993
    641.5'55—dc20   92-33498
                                                              CIP

Printed in the United States of America
First Edition

1   2   3   4   5   6   7   8   9   10

Book Design by Barbara Cohen Aronica.

CONTENTS

Whether plated, passed or just picked up on the fly, these easy hors d'oeuvres include Baked Goat Cheese with Hazelnuts, Coconut Shrimp, Eggplant Sandwiches and Nachos.

Fast soups everyone will think are from scratch range from starters, such as Almond Squash Soup and Taco Soup, to main dishes in a bowl—New England Clam Chowder and Hearty Ham and Bean Soup.

First-course and main-course salads as well as side salads are suggested here. Some tempting combinations include Avocado and Crabmeat with Watercress Mayonnaise, Black Bean Salad Olé, Spinach Salad with Mandarin Oranges and Minted Pea Salad.

4. CHICKEN, TURKEY, BEEF, PORK AND LAMB 67

All the meats are covered here, in a dazzling variety of 10-minute ways: Broiled Chicken with Tequila and Lime, Mustard-Sauced Pork Chops, Skillet Beef Stew in Red Wine, Apricot-Sauced Chicken and Butterflied Steaks with Sun-Dried Tomatoes and Mushrooms, to name a few.

5. FISH AND SHELLFISH 93

Shellfish is naturally fast cooking, so there's lots of room for creativity. Some of the simple and delicious ideas in this chapter are Broiled Fillet of Sole with Green Olive Paste, Crispy Potato Crust Trout, Spicy Garlic Shrimp and Quick Salmon Croquettes.

6. PASTA 115

Make the sauce while the pasta is cooking and you'll come up with such tempting recipes as Linguine with Clam Sauce, Pasta Shells with Corn and Chicken, Fettuccine with Fresh Asparagus and Ham, and Fusilli with Sautéed Eggplant and Feta Cheese.

INTRODUCTION

I'm a strong advocate for families eating dinner together. Even so, I know it won't be easy to save the family dinner from extinction while also juggling adults' work schedules with children's homework and a dozen other activities in a dozen different locations.

Not enough time is everyone's biggest problem. Even single working people complain that finding time to cook meals is difficult. Dinnertime is a lot like body weight. If you're not diligent, it creeps up on you. It's impossible to get a delicious, nourishing dinner on the table at a reasonable hour, such as 6:30 P.M., when you don't get home from work until 7 P.M.

The idea for this book was born the harried day that the four members of our family sat down to eat at 9 P.M. (about my 8-year-old's bedtime) for the second pizza in nearly as many days. It's not that we don't know what to do. (In our family, one parent teaches culinary professionals how to manage, the other is a newspaper food editor with a master's degree in home economics.) What became clear over that vegetarian pizza was that we desperately needed to adopt some new cooking strategies.

"How fast can we make dinner?" is the question my husband and I asked ourselves. Is it possible to create a delicious dish from basic ingredients, not a packaged microwave marvel, in as few as 10 minutes. What if we limited ourselves to five ingredients—not counting salt and pepper? A number of time-saving cookbooks have been published, but many of them contain recipes with so many ingredients that just the shopping and assembling appear daunting.

The most interesting things happened as we became immersed in the *5 in 10* project—we started eating more healthfully, and we began saving money.

The 5 in 10 Cookbook wasn't meant to be a diet book. Many of the recipes, however, turned out to contain relatively little fat. Why waste one of the 5 ingredients on fat when herbs and spices contribute so much more pizzazz and flavor?

Although saving time was our goal, we found that we saved a fortune when we stopped bringing in carryout a couple of nights a week and started limiting the number of ingredients we purchased. It's amazing how much money all those little extras previously added to the total on the supermarket checkout tape.

We also discovered how many good "convenient" basic ingredients are readily available today. Canned beans, for example, allowed us to whip together "homemade" black bean soup in six minutes. With prepared chunky marinara sauce and fresh pasta, a satisfying dinner is only eight minutes away. Roasted, peeled sweet red peppers save hours previously spent charring and tugging reluctant skin off peppers. Washed, ready-to-use spinach is another terrific timesaver.

With a carefully stocked pantry, dozens of delicious dishes are possible in 10 minutes or less. A versatile *5 in 10* cupboard contains a number of canned foods: both chicken and beef broth for quick soups, salmon for crispy croquettes, sardines for pasta sauces and quick appetizers, cream-style corn to make hearty corn chowder, pitted olives to puree as a topping for grilled fish, and a variety of tomatoes. Except during a few hot summer months, canned tomatoes generally taste fresher—and more flavorful— than fresh tomatoes.

In addition, a well-stocked *5 in 10* pantry includes a selection of dried pastas, quick-cooking rice and several herb blends, including fines herbes and herbes de Provence. A note about seasoning: Specific amounts of herbs and spices are listed in the recipes, but it's always best to season to your own taste. The same rule applies to salt and pepper.

This project gave us new respect for the advantages of our $200 popcorn popper—that is, our microwave oven. Using it as a tool, in tandem with other appliances, to heat vegetables and to melt butter and chocolate saved precious time. A food processor, blender, small electric chopper and a garlic press are all helpful to people who aren't magicians with their knives. And, speaking about knives, it's important that they be sharp and that you use the right one for the job. For example, it's much faster to chop or slice an onion with a large, sharp chef's knife than with a tiny paring knife.

Professional chefs who regularly prepare dishes *à la minute,* that is, "quickly, at the very last minute," cook over high heat. Using that same high heat is how I was able to create such a variety of recipes in 10 minutes or less. To be successful, however, it is essential to use a good, heavy frying pan. It is also important to be single-minded and keep a watchful eye on what you're cooking. If the food begins to brown too quickly, just reduce the heat slightly.

There are some other tips to playing the "beat the dinner bell" game: First, read the recipe completely through before you start. Second, get out all of the ingredients and equipment before you begin working. The professionals call it preparing the *mise en place,* or getting everything together. Don't set the 10-minute timer until you know exactly what you will be doing. Some of the recipes, particularly the fish and seafood recipes and soups, are completed well ahead of the time allowed. Others take the full 10 minutes.

The 164 recipes that follow prove that it's possible to get a homemade dinner on the table in less time than it takes to pick up a take-out pizza. Family dinners may be saved from extinction yet.

1 APPETIZERS AND SNACKS

It's amazing how many unusual appetizers and snacks are possible in 10 minutes. Flour tortillas are great to keep on hand for quick quesadillas. Pita bread rounds make marvelous "homemade" crackers. Just brush them lightly with an orange-scented butter, sprinkle generously with grated cheese and pop under the broiler until crisp and golden brown.

Everyone loves dips. Both the zesty garbanzo dip and smoked fish spread recipes are delicious with fresh vegetables as well as with crackers.

Many of the recipes in this chapter make elegant first courses. Blini Topped with Smoked Salmon is made possible in 10 minutes by using buckwheat pancake mix thinned with beer. Baked Goat Cheese with Hazelnuts is always a favorite, and it's so simple. Just coat a round of goat cheese with chopped nuts, drizzle with olive oil and bake about five minutes, until heated through. Another delicious first course is Sage and Cornmeal–Crusted Jack Cheese. Serve the bubbly cheese with mango chutney and warm tortilla chips.

With these ideas from *5 in 10,* it's not necessary to always resort to potato chips and pretzels.

BAKED GOAT CHEESE WITH HAZELNUTS

This is a standard in our home. Sometimes we coat the cheese with bread crumbs. Other times we use chopped nuts. When we bake a larger round, we serve it with toasted slices of French or Italian bread as an appetizer. Smaller rounds of the warm cheese are delicious served on mixed greens for a salad course.

12 thin slices of baguette or narrow French bread
3 tablespoons extra virgin olive oil
1 round (6 ounces) herbed goat cheese
¾ cup finely chopped hazelnuts or walnuts

1. Preheat the broiler. If your oven is separate, preheat to 375 degrees F. Arrange the slices of bread on a baking sheet. Broil 3 to 4 inches from the heat until lightly toasted, about 1 minute. Turn the slices of bread over, brush lightly with olive oil and broil until brown on the other side, 1 to 2 minutes.

2. Coat the goat cheese all over with the chopped nuts. Press any extra nuts into the cheese. Place the cheese in a small baking dish. Drizzle the remaining olive oil over the cheese and bake at 375 degrees until heated through, about 5 minutes.

3. To serve, spread the baked cheese on the croutons.

4 SERVINGS

EGGPLANT SANDWICHES

Slices of eggplant form the "bread" in these savory sandwiches.
Serve them hot or at room temperature.

1 medium-size eggplant (about 1 pound)
6 thin slices of Monterey Jack or Cheddar cheese
3 slices of cooked ham
½ cup flour
2 tablespoons oil
   Salt and freshly ground black pepper

1. Trim away the stem end of the eggplant. Then cut a thin slice
from the 2 opposite long sides so the eggplant can lie flat. Cut the
remaining eggplant lengthwise into 6 slices about ¼ inch thick.
(Discard the end slices or reserve for another use.) Place 3 of the
eggplant slices on a flat surface. Cover each with a slice of cheese,
then with a slice of ham and finally a second slice of cheese. Top
with the remaining eggplant slices to form sandwiches.

2. Dip the eggplant sandwiches in the flour. Shake off any excess.

3. Heat the oil in a large frying pan over moderately high heat.
Be sure the oil is hot before cooking the eggplant. Cook the
eggplant sandwiches, turning once, until they are well browned
on both sides, about 6 to 8 minutes. Season with salt and pepper
to taste before cutting into 1½- to 2-inch squares to serve.

8 APPETIZER SERVINGS

FRESH FIGS WITH HAM MOUSSE

When fresh figs are in season we eat them as often as possible—
out of hand, brushed with honey and grilled, or topped with a
light ham mousse for an easy hors d'oeuvre. If fresh figs aren't
available, try the ham mousse on dried apricot halves.

6 ripe fresh Black Mission figs
¼ pound cooked ham
1 package (3 ounces) cream cheese
1 tablespoon lemon juice
1 tablespoon sliced almonds

1. Rinse the figs and dry. Cut them in half and arrange the halves
on a platter.

2. Cut the ham in pieces and place them in a food processor.
Pulse several times to chop the ham. Add the cream cheese and
lemon juice and process a minute or so until the mixture is
smooth.

3. Place the almond slices in a small, dry skillet. Cook over
medium-high heat, shaking the pan frequently, for 2 to 3 minutes,
until toasted. Be careful they don't burn.

4. Spoon the ham mousse onto each fig half. Sprinkle a few slices
of toasted almonds on top.

12 SERVINGS

HERRING APPLE BOATS

Crisp cucumber, tart apple and crunchy bits of celery combine with creamy herring in this delicious and healthful appetizer. You may want to use the small pickling Kirby cucumbers when they are in season.

1 jar (6 ounces) herring in cream sauce
1 small Red Delicious apple
1 small celery rib
2 medium-size cucumbers
1 tablespoon finely chopped parsley

1. Cut the herring into ¼-inch dice and place in a bowl. Core the apple, cut it into ¼-inch dice and add to the herring. Finely chop the celery and stir it into the herring and apple mixture.

2. Peel the cucumbers. Slice them in half lengthwise and scoop out the seeds, using the end of a vegetable peeler or the tip of a spoon.

3. Spoon the herring and apple mixture into the cucumber halves. Sprinkle with parsley and cut into 1½-inch pieces to offer as a pick-up appetizer. To serve as a first course, slice the cucumbers and arrange them on small plates. Spoon the herring and apple mixture on top and garnish with the parsley.

6 TO 8 SERVINGS

HUMMUS

Spread this zippy bean dip on pita bread triangles or use as a dip for crisp, raw vegetables. Carrot and green pepper strips and radishes are especially nice.

Tahini, or ground sesame seed paste, is becoming a staple on supermarket shelves. Occasionally, when you first open the jar, you may notice that it has separated like natural peanut butter. If so, just stir until smooth.

1 can (15½ ounces) garbanzo beans (chick-peas)
1 garlic clove, peeled
¼ cup tahini (sesame seed paste)
⅓ cup lemon juice
¼ teaspoon ground cumin

1. Drain the garbanzo beans. Rinse them under cold water, then drain well.

2. With the food processor running, drop the garlic clove through the feed tube. Process for 30 seconds, or until the garlic is finely chopped.

3. Add the garbanzo beans and pulse several times. Add the tahini, lemon juice and cumin to the bean mixture and puree until the dip is smooth.

MAKES ABOUT 1½ CUPS

NACHOS

A favorite quick lunch or snack, nachos are often fried in butter or oil. We prefer to bake them in a hot oven and save all those calories.

 2 flour tortillas, 7 to 8 inches in diameter
½ cup prepared or homemade salsa
 1 can (4 ounces) diced mild green chiles
 1 cup shredded Monterey Jack cheese (4 ounces)

1. Preheat the oven to 425 degrees F. Place the tortillas on a large baking sheet. Spread the salsa evenly over each.

2. Drain the chiles and scatter over the salsa. Top with the cheese.

3. Bake for about 8 minutes, or until the tortillas are crisp and the cheese is melted. Cut into wedges and serve.

2 SERVINGS

OYSTERS WITH BACON AND SPINACH

This recipe makes an interesting and elegant first course for a sit-down dinner. Or the oysters can be speared with toothpicks and passed as a hot hors d'oeuvre.

18 thin slices of bacon
 2 jars (10 ounces each) shucked oysters in their own juices
18 large leaves of fresh ready-to-use spinach
¼ cup Pernod

1. Place bacon on a plate lined with microwave-safe paper toweling and microwave on High for 3 minutes.

2. Preheat the broiler. While the bacon is cooking, drain the oysters and wrap a spinach leaf around each oyster.

3. Next, wrap a slice of precooked bacon around the spinach. Then drizzle about 2 teaspoons Pernod on top of each oyster to wet the spinach.

4. Arrange the oysters seam side down on a broiler pan and broil 3 to 4 inches from the heat for 2 to 4 minutes, until the bacon is crisp and the oysters are hot. Serve immediately.

6 SERVINGS

ORANGE PARMESAN PITA CHIPS

½ cup butter
6 pita breads (10-ounce package)
⅓ cup undiluted orange juice concentrate
¾ cup grated Parmesan or Romano cheese
½ cup chopped fresh parsley

1. Preheat the broiler. Cut the butter in pieces and place them in a microwave-safe bowl. Heat on High until the butter is melted, about 1 minute.

2. Meanwhile, trim a thin slice off the edge of 1 pita bread. Slip a thin-bladed knife into the opening and separate the bread into 2 thin rounds. Repeat with the remaining pita breads. Place 2 of the halves on a baking sheet.

3. When the butter is melted, stir in the orange juice concentrate. Brush the pita lightly with the orange butter. Sprinkle 1 tablespoon cheese and 2 teaspoons parsley over each pita half.

4. Place under the broiler, 3 to 4 inches from the heat, and broil until the cheese is bubbly and the pita is crisp, 1 to 1½ minutes. Cut each half into quarters to serve. Repeat with remaining ingredients.

48 PITA CHIPS

HOT SAUSAGE AND SWEET RED PEPPER BITES

You may want to double the recipe because these spicy sausage bites usually disappear in a hurry. Using prepared roasted and peeled sweet red peppers makes this easily a 10-minute recipe.

½ pound andouille sausage (2 links) or hot or
    sweet Italian sausage
2 tablespoons honey mustard or horseradish mustard
2 whole roasted red peppers

1. Preheat the broiler. Cut the sausage, crosswise on a diagonal, into ½-inch-thick slices. Spread each slice of sausage with about ¼ teaspoon of mustard and arrange on a broiler rack. Broil until heated through and brown at the edges, about 5 minutes.

2. While the sausage is cooking, cut the red pepper into 20 pieces approximately 1½ inches square. Remove the sausage slices from the oven when they are done and drain them briefly on paper towels. Top each slice with a red pepper square and serve hot.

MAKES ABOUT 20 APPETIZERS

SAGE AND CORNMEAL—CRUSTED JACK CHEESE

Serve this appetizer as soon as it turns golden brown, so the cheese is still melted. Spread the hot sage-flavored cheese on unsalted tortilla chips. Mango chutney makes a nice accompaniment.

1 wheel (1 pound) garlic-flavored Jack cheese
1 egg
1 cup yellow cornmeal
2 tablespoons ground sage
1 cup oil for frying

1. Cut the wheel of cheese into 12 wedges. Break the egg into a shallow bowl. Beat until blended. Combine the cornmeal and sage in a shallow pie plate.

2. Heat the oil in a large frying pan. While the oil is heating, dip the wedges of cheese into the egg, then dredge in the cornmeal, turning to coat all sides.

3. Fry the coated wedges of cheese in the hot oil, turning to brown all sides, for about 2 minutes. Remove the cheese with a slotted spoon to small plates and serve immediately along with tortilla chips.

12 SERVINGS

SHRIMP IN TARRAGON VINAIGRETTE WITH BELGIAN ENDIVE

Either spoon the marinated shrimp onto the endive leaves for a pick-up appetizer or arrange the endive leaves on plates and then top with the shrimp for an easy first course.

2 tablespoons extra virgin olive oil
1 tablespoon tarragon-flavored white wine vinegar plus
    1 teaspoon chopped tarragon leaves (from the vinegar)
¼ pound cooked shelled baby shrimp
    1 tablespoon chopped drained pimiento (optional)
2 heads Belgian endive

1. In a medium bowl, whisk together the oil, vinegar and chopped tarragon leaves. When the mixture is well blended, fold in the shrimp and the pimiento, if you're using it.

2. Separate the heads of endive into individual leaves. Arrange them on a platter. Spoon about 1 teaspoon of the shrimp mixture onto each endive leaf and serve.

6 SERVINGS

SHRIMP WITH SAMBUCA
AND PROSCIUTTO

A faint anise flavor is perfect with shrimp. In this quick appetizer, shrimp are marinated in sambuca, a licorice-flavored Italian liqueur, for about 5 minutes, then wrapped with paper-thin slices of prosciutto (or another cured ham or slices of partially cooked bacon) and broiled until the shrimp turn pink and the ham gets crisp.

1 pound large shrimp (18 to 20 per pound), shelled and
   deveined
½ cup sambuca or Pernod
9 to 10 thin slices of prosciutto

1. Place the shrimp in a medium bowl. Pour the sambuca over them. Marinate about 5 minutes, stirring occasionally. Meanwhile, cut prosciutto slices in half.

2. Preheat the broiler. Wrap the prosciutto around the shrimp. Arrange on a broiler pan. Broil 3 to 4 inches from the heat, turning once, until the shrimp are pink and curled, about 3 to 5 minutes. Serve warm.

6 SERVINGS

COCONUT SHRIMP

Sweet shrimp coated with crispy coconut make a festive appetizer. To save time, buy the shrimp already cleaned, shelled and deveined.

    1 cup flour
    1 cup beer
    1 pound medium shrimp (24 to a pound), shelled and
       deveined
    1 package (14 ounces) shredded coconut
1½ cups oil for frying

1. Whisk together the flour and beer until the batter is smooth. Dip the shrimp into the beer batter, then dip them into the shredded coconut, turning to coat all sides.

2. Pour the oil into a large, deep frying pan and heat over high heat to 375 degrees F. To be sure the oil is hot enough, drop a shred of coconut into the oil; it should begin sizzling immediately.

3. Fry the shrimp in 2 or 3 batches without crowding, turning them occasionally, until they are cooked through and curled and the coconut is golden brown, 2 to 3 minutes. Remove the shrimp with a slotted spoon and drain on paper towels. Serve hot.

8 SERVINGS (3 SHRIMP EACH)

BAY SHRIMP COCKTAIL

Serve this refreshing first course or appetizer in stemmed wineglasses, if you have them. This recipe is especially nice on warm days.

¼ pound cooked baby shrimp (shrimp meat)
1 can (14½ ounces) peeled tomatoes, diced in juice
4 green onions
1 ripe avocado
½ teaspoon hot pepper sauce
¼ teaspoon salt

1. Place the shrimp in a bowl. Stir in the tomatoes with their juice.

2. Trim away the root ends of the green onions and rinse them. Cut the onions in half lengthwise, then slice thinly.

3. Peel and dice the avocado. Gently fold the avocado chunks and the green onions into the shrimp and tomato mixture.

4. Season the shrimp cocktail with the hot sauce and salt. Spoon into stemmed goblets. Serve at once or refrigerate until chilled.

6 SERVINGS

SMOKED FISH SPREAD

Spread this zesty mixture on miniature bagels, crisp crackers or slices of cucumber.

½ pound smoked cod fillets
1 container (8 ounces) whipped cream cheese
1½ tablespoons lemon juice
1 tablespoon plus 1 teaspoon prepared white horseradish
4 green onions

1. Remove the skin from the fish along with any little bones. Place the fish in a food processor. Pulse several times to chop it. Add the cream cheese, lemon juice and horseradish and process about 30 seconds longer, until the mixture is well combined.

2. Cut the root ends off the green onions, and finely slice them. Add the onions to the smoked fish mixture and process several seconds, just until they are mixed in.

3. Serve immediately with crackers or refrigerate to serve later.

MAKES 2 CUPS

BLINI TOPPED WITH SMOKED SALMON

1 cup buckwheat pancake mix
1 cup beer
4 teaspoons oil
¼ pound smoked salmon, thinly sliced
⅓ cup sour cream

1. Preheat a griddle or large, heavy skillet over moderately high heat. Combine the buckwheat pancake mix, beer and 1 teaspoon of the oil. Whisk until the batter is smooth.

2. When the griddle is hot (a few drops of water sprinkled on the surface will sputter and dance about), brush lightly with some of the remaining oil. Pour about 1 tablespoon of batter per blini onto the griddle. When bubbles appear on the top of the blini and the bottom is golden brown, 1 to 2 minutes, turn over and cook the other side until spotted brown, 30 to 60 seconds. Repeat with the remaining batter. Arrange the blini on a platter as they are cooked.

3. Cut smoked salmon into 18 pieces. Top each blini with a piece of smoked salmon and a dab of sour cream. Serve immediately.

6 SERVINGS (3 BLINI PER SERVING)

BRUSCHETTA WITH SARDINES

Rub slices of grilled bread with a clove of garlic and then drizzle on fruity olive oil for a wonderful snack. Adding sardines, an often overlooked treat, and red onion rings gilds the lily, so to speak. Although you can toast the bread under the broiler, it's even better grilled over charcoal. This is a recipe to remember next time you light the barbecue.

⅓ of a baguette (narrow French bread), about
   7 inches in length
1 garlic clove
2 tablespoons extra virgin olive oil
1 can (3¾ ounces) sardines packed in olive oil
½ small red onion

1. Slice the bread horizontally into 2 long halves. Place the bread, cut side up, on a baking sheet. Broil 3 to 4 inches from the heat until the bread is golden brown, 1 to 2 minutes.

2. Peel and cut the garlic in half. Rub the toasted bread with the cut side of the garlic. Then drizzle on the olive oil.

3. Arrange the sardines on top of the bread. Peel the red onion, then thinly slice and separate into rings. Scatter onion rings on top of the sardines. Cut each slice of bread into quarters and serve.

8 SERVINGS

MINI MANGO CORN MUFFINS

Cooks in a hurry will find it worthwhile to invest in miniature muffin tins. Compared to regular-size muffins that take 15 to 20 minutes to bake, bite-size muffins are done in just 10 minutes. Mango chutney adds a sweet touch to this recipe. For an easy appetizer, spread a mixture of chopped smoked ham and whipped cream cheese over the muffins.

1 cup milk
1 cup mango chutney
2 large eggs
1 cup yellow cornmeal
1 cup buttermilk baking and pancake mix

1. Preheat oven to 425 degrees F. Lightly oil 3 dozen miniature muffin cups (preferably nonstick) or spray with nonstick vegetable coating.

2. Place the milk, chutney and eggs in a food processor. Pulse several times to break up the chutney. Add the cornmeal and pancake mix and pulse several more times until the mixture is smooth.

3. Fill the muffin cups ¾ full, using about 1 tablespoon of batter in each cup. Bake 10 minutes, or until lightly browned around rim and edges begin to pull away from sides of pan. Serve warm.

36 MINIATURE MUFFINS

QUESADILLA CAKE

Let your imagination come up with other ideas for filling this tortilla stack. Some ideas include: chopped tomatoes, shredded cooked chicken, cooked ground beef, sliced olives, sour cream and shredded Cheddar cheese.

1 can (15 ounces) black beans
4 flour tortillas, 7 to 8 inches in diameter
1 can (16 ounces) refried beans
1½ cups tomato and green chile salsa
1 package (6 ounces) shredded Monterey Jack cheese (1½ cups)

1. Preheat the oven to 500 degrees F. Drain the black beans. Rinse them under cold running water, then drain again.

2. Place a tortilla on a lightly oiled baking sheet. Spread one-third of the refried beans over the tortilla. Then sprinkle on one-third of the black beans, one-third of the salsa and one-third of the cheese. Place another tortilla on top and repeat the layering, using half the remaining ingredients. Add another tortilla and repeat. Top the stack with a flour tortilla.

3. Bake in a hot oven for 8 to 10 minutes, until the "cake" is heated through and the outer tortillas are crisp. Cut into wedges to serve.

6 TO 8 SERVINGS

THE 5 IN 10 COOKBOOK • 21

Strawberries Wrapped in Prosciutto

Sweet, juicy fresh fruit wrapped in paper-thin slices of salty prosciutto is a popular hors d'oeuvre. Although prosciutto and melon are the classic combination, we've found that the cured ham goes especially well with strawberries.

12 large ripe strawberries with the leaves still
   attached, if possible
12 paper-thin slices of prosciutto

1. Rinse and dry the strawberries.

2. Fold the top edge of prosciutto (with the thin border of fat) over to double the thickness of the slice. Wrap a slice of prosciutto around a strawberry with the white edge of fat showing on the outside. Repeat with remaining prosciutto and berries. Serve at room temperature or chilled.

12 SERVINGS

SPICY WALNUTS

Don't say we didn't warn you that these salty, spiced nuts can be addictive. If they aren't all gobbled up as snacks, toss some over salads or float on top of soup.

    2 tablespoons vegetable oil
 1½ tablespoons crumbled dried thyme leaves
   ½ teaspoon hot pepper sauce
    1 pound shelled walnut or pecan halves (4 cups)
   ½ teaspoon salt

1. Preheat the oven to 425 degrees F. In a 1½- to 2-quart bowl, combine the oil, thyme and hot sauce. Add the nuts and stir gently until the nuts are well coated with the oil and seasonings.

2. Place the nuts in a single layer on a large baking sheet. Scrape any oil or thyme that remains in the bowl over the nuts. Then sprinkle on the salt.

3. Bake for 8 to 10 minutes, until the nuts are toasted. Check occasionally to be sure they don't get too brown.

MAKES 1 QUART

2 SOUPS AND CHOWDERS

Our happiest *5 in 10* discovery was dispelling the myth that richly flavored, homemade-tasting soups must be simmered slowly over a long period of time. Not true. Chunky Corn and Ham Chowder, creamy smooth Black Bean Soup, hearty New England Clam Chowder, a filling Minute Minestrone and savory Parmesan Pumpkin Soup are representative of the many great "homemade" soups that are ready to serve in 10 minutes.

Chicken, beef or vegetable broth provides the base for many of the recipes that follow. While full-flavored homemade stock is ideal, there's nothing wrong with using canned broth for a convenient substitute. Many people prefer the flavor and lower salt content of reduced-sodium brands.

If there are any leftovers, all of these soups store well, several days in the refrigerator or several months in the freezer. Just reheat quickly in the microwave for an easy lunch or a nutritious hot snack.

ALMOND SQUASH SOUP

For more flavor, toast the almond slices in a 350-degree oven for 3 to 5 minutes, until fragrant and golden brown. Watch carefully, because nuts can burn easily.

1 package (10 ounces) frozen cooked squash
1 can (14½ ounces) chicken broth
1 tablespoon firmly packed brown sugar
1 tablespoon butter
¼ cup sliced almonds

1. Thaw the squash in a microwave oven on High for 3 minutes.

2. Place the squash and chicken broth in a medium saucepan. Bring to a simmer over medium-high heat. When the soup is hot, after about 5 minutes, stir in the brown sugar and butter until melted.

3. Pour into soup bowls and garnish with the sliced almonds.

4 SERVINGS

BLACK BEAN SOUP

For more texture, we puree only 2 cans of the black beans. If you prefer a completely smooth soup, puree all of the beans and add a half cup more stock. Sprigs of cilantro would be an attractive garnish in addition to the splashes of yogurt.

3 cans (15 ounces each) black beans
1 cup beef or chicken stock
¾ cup dry red wine
1 tablespoon chili powder
¼ cup plain yogurt

1. Puree 2 cans of the beans with their liquid in a food processor or blender. Pour the bean puree into a nonreactive, medium saucepan. Drain the remaining can of beans and add them to the pan.

2. Stir in the stock, wine and chili powder. Bring the mixture to a simmer over medium heat, stirring occasionally, about 5 minutes.

3. Stir the yogurt until smooth. Ladle the hot soup into soup bowls. Garnish each serving by drizzling on about 2 teaspoons yogurt.

6 SERVINGS

CHICKEN NOODLE SOUP

This homemade soup will bring back childhood memories.

2 cans (14½ ounces each) chicken broth
4 ounces thin egg noodles
1 cup finely shredded carrots (2 medium carrots)
1 whole skinless, boneless chicken breast (about 8 ounces)
¼ cup chopped fresh parsley

1. Pour the chicken broth into a medium saucepan. Stir in the noodles and carrots. Bring to a simmer over high heat, about 2 minutes.

2. Meanwhile, cut the chicken breast into ½-inch dice. Add the chicken pieces to the soup, reduce the heat to a simmer and continue to cook until the noodles and carrots are tender and the chicken is done, 4 to 6 minutes longer. Sprinkle with the parsley and serve.

4 SERVINGS

CHUNKY CORN AND HAM CHOWDER

If you have a leftover boiled potato, dice it up and add to this satisfying corn soup to make it even heartier.

    2 cans (17 ounces each) cream-style corn
    2 cans (14½ ounces each) chicken broth
    1 cup finely diced cooked smoked ham (about ¼ pound)
    1 cup heavy cream
    ½ cup minced fresh chives

1. Pour the corn and the chicken broth into a medium saucepan. Stir in the diced ham and bring to a simmer over medium heat, stirring occasionally, about 5 minutes.

2. Stir in the cream and heat through.

3. Ladle the hot soup into bowls and garnish with the chives.

6 SERVINGS

NEW ENGLAND CLAM CHOWDER

Here's a quick recipe for making a tasty shellfish soup.

1 can (1 pound) boiled new potatoes
2 cans (10 ounces each) baby clams in juice
2 bottles (7⅞ ounces each) clam juice
2 tablespoons flour (preferably quick dissolving)
1 cup milk

1. Drain the potatoes. Cut them into ½-inch dice.

2. In a medium saucepan, combine the potatoes, clams and their juices and the clam juice. Bring to a simmer over medium-high heat.

3. Dissolve the flour in the milk. Gradually stir into the hot soup. Continue cooking, stirring, until the soup boils and thickens, about 3 minutes. Pour into bowls and serve.

6 SERVINGS

CREAM OF BROCCOLI SOUP

Tarragon can be substituted for the lemon zest if you like. Herbed croutons are an alternative garnish instead of the cheese.

1 package (1 pound) frozen broccoli
2 cans (14½ ounces each) chicken broth
1 cup milk
1 teaspoon lemon zest (grated outer rind of lemon)
1 cup shredded Cheddar cheese (about 4 ounces)

1. Place the broccoli and chicken broth in a nonreactive, medium saucepan. Bring to boil over high heat. Reduce the heat to medium and simmer, partially covered, until the broccoli is tender, about 5 minutes. Puree the mixture in a blender or food processor until smooth.

2. Return the broccoli puree to the saucepan. Stir in the milk and lemon zest and heat through. Ladle the hot soup into serving bowls and garnish with a generous sprinkling of cheese. Pass the remaining cheese on the side.

4 TO 6 SERVINGS

CREAM OF SPINACH SOUP WITH PEARS

Diced pears are a surprise ingredient in this rich, flavorful soup. It makes a terrific first course.

```
   1 package (10 ounces) frozen chopped spinach
   1 pear
   1 can (14½ ounces) chicken broth
1½ cups half-and-half or milk
   1 teaspoon ground cumin
```

1. Place the spinach in a 1-quart microwave-safe casserole. Cover and microwave on High for 4 minutes.

2. While the spinach is cooking, peel the pear, remove the core and cut into ½-inch dice.

3. Puree the cooked spinach and any accumulated juices in a food processor. Pour the spinach puree into a medium, nonreactive saucepan. Stir in the diced pear, chicken broth, half-and-half and ground cumin. Cook over medium-high heat, stirring, until heated through, about 4 minutes. Serve immediately.

4 SERVINGS

CREAMY TOMATO SOUP WITH AVOCADO

Slices of pale green avocado add delicate flavor and beautiful color contrast as a garnish for this creamy tomato soup. Who would guess that this fresh-tasting soup is ready in 5 minutes?

1 can (28 ounces) crushed tomatoes with added puree
1 cup chicken stock
1 can (12 ounces) unsweetened evaporated milk
1 teaspoon dried thyme leaves
1 ripe avocado

1. Place the tomatoes with their juices in a nonreactive, medium saucepan. Stir in the chicken stock and evaporated milk.

2. Crush the dried thyme with your fingers and add it to soup. (If you have fresh thyme leaves, just stir them in.)

3. Bring the soup to a simmer over medium heat, about 5 minutes, stirring occasionally.

4. Cut the avocado in half. Remove the pit and cut each half lengthwise into 9 thin slices, removing the peel.

5. Spoon the hot soup into soup bowls. Garnish each serving with 3 avocado slices.

6 SERVINGS

CUCUMBER SOUP WITH TOMATOES

Chopped tomatoes add a pretty color and nice flavor to this refreshing soup.

 4 medium-size cucumbers
 1 can (14½ ounces) chicken broth
 1 cup chopped ripe tomato (fresh or canned)
 ¼ cup fresh lime juice
 ¼ teaspoon cayenne pepper

1. Peel the cucumbers. Quarter them lengthwise. Remove the seeds with the tip of a spoon. Puree 2 of the cucumbers with the chicken stock in a blender or food processor. Pour the cucumber puree into a large serving bowl.

2. Thinly slice the remaining 2 cucumbers. Add the cucumber slices, tomato, lime juice and cayenne pepper to the cucumber puree. Stir gently until combined. Serve immediately or chill and serve later.

4 TO 6 SERVINGS

CURRIED CARROT SOUP

Curry powder adds a lively flavor to creamy carrot soup.

1 package (1 pound) frozen carrots
1 can (14½ ounces) chicken broth
1 cup milk
1 tablespoon curry powder
½ teaspoon ground cumin

1. Place the carrots and chicken broth in a medium saucepan. Bring to a boil over medium-high heat. Reduce the heat to medium and simmer until the carrots are tender, about 6 minutes.

2. Transfer the carrots and stock to a food processor or blender and puree until smooth. Return the carrot puree to the saucepan. Stir in the milk, curry powder and ground cumin. Cook, stirring occasionally, until heated through.

4 SERVINGS

GUATEMALAN AVOCADO SOUP

We call this Guatemalan Avocado Soup because the friend who shared the recipe with us first tasted a similar soup during a trip to Central America. If you have any salty tortilla chips around, sprinkle a few on top. Sliced ripe olives are also a nice addition scattered on top of this hearty soup.

1 large garlic clove
1 small onion
1 can (14½ ounces) beef broth
1 can (16 ounces) refried beans
1 small ripe avocado

1. In a food processor or blender, mince the garlic and onion. Heat about ½ cup of the broth in a medium saucepan. Add the garlic and onion and simmer until the onion is translucent, about 2 minutes. Stir in the remaining beef broth and the refried beans, blending well.

2. While the soup is heating through, mash the avocado with a fork. To serve, ladle the hot soup into individual soup plates. Top each serving with a dollop of pureed avocado.

3 SERVINGS

HEARTY HAM AND BEAN SOUP

If you have any cooked potatoes or other leftover vegetables, by all means add them to the pot. For a thicker consistency, puree half the beans in a food processor before adding them to the soup.

2 cans (15 ounces each) cannellini beans
1 can (14½ ounces) stewed tomatoes
1 ham slice, about ¼ inch thick (6 to 8 ounces)
1 can (14½ ounces) beef broth
2 fresh limes or 1 lemon

1. Drain the beans and rinse well under cold running water; drain again. Coarsely cut up the tomatoes, reserving all the juices. Cut the ham into ¼-inch dice.

2. In a nonreactive, medium saucepan, combine the beans, tomatoes with their juices, ham and beef broth. Bring to a simmer over medium heat, stirring occasionally. Partially cover and simmer for 5 minutes.

3. Squeeze the juice from 1 lime or ½ lemon into the soup. Cut the remaining lime or lemon half into wedges. Serve the soup hot, garnished with a lime or lemon wedge.

4 TO 6 SERVINGS

ITALIAN WINTER SOUP

Pasta and beef make a popular Italian combo that's a favorite of children of all ages.

 2 cans (14½ ounces each) beef broth
½ cup elbow macaroni
 1 pound lean ground beef
 1 can (15 ounces) red kidney beans
 1 cup chunky spaghetti sauce

1. Pour the beef broth and macaroni into a nonreactive, medium saucepan. Bring to a boil over high heat and cook, stirring occasionally, until the macaroni is tender, about 5 minutes.

2. Meanwhile, cook the ground beef in a frying pan, stirring to break up large clumps, until the meat is brown; drain off any fat.

3. Drain the beans, reserving the liquid. Puree 1 cup of the beans with all of the reserved liquid from the can in a blender or food processor. When the macaroni is tender, stir the pureed beans, whole beans, cooked meat and spaghetti sauce into the pot. Heat through and serve.

6 SERVINGS

MINUTE MINESTRONE

For extra protein and flavor, top each serving of this hearty vegetable soup with a drift of grated Parmesan or Romano cheese.

3 cans (14½ ounces each) beef broth
1 cup elbow macaroni
3 cups loosely packed fresh ready-to-use spinach leaves
1 can (15 ounces) cannellini beans
1 cup chopped tomatoes (fresh or canned)

1. Pour the beef broth into a nonreactive, medium saucepan. Stir in the elbow macaroni. Bring to a boil over medium-high heat. Cook, stirring occasionally, until the macaroni is tender, about 4 to 6 minutes. Meanwhile, rinse the spinach leaves.

2. Drain the beans and stir them into the soup. Add the chopped tomatoes and heat through. Just before serving, add the spinach. Ladle into soup bowls and serve.

6 TO 8 SERVINGS

OYSTER BISQUE WITH SPINACH

This is a quick version of a classic soup. For a more elegant presentation, ladle into flameproof soup bowls, float lightly whipped cream on top of each portion and run under the broiler for a minute or so to brown lightly.

1 package (10 ounces) ready-to-use fresh spinach
2 tablespoons butter
1 jar (10 ounces) shucked oysters in their own juices
1 cup chicken broth
½ cup heavy cream

1. Rinse the spinach. Melt the butter in a nonreactive, medium saucepan. Add the spinach and cook, stirring, until the spinach is tender, about 3 minutes.

2. Pour the spinach and any juices in the pan into a blender or food processor and puree until smooth. Add the oysters and their juices and puree again. Pour the mixture into the saucepan, stir in the chicken broth and heat through, about 2 minutes.

3. Stir the cream into the soup and simmer for 1 minute longer. Ladle into soup plates and serve at once.

4 SERVINGS

PARMESAN PUMPKIN SOUP

Parmesan cheese adds a nice textural contrast to this otherwise creamy soup.

  1 can (16 ounces) solid-packed pumpkin
  1 can (14½ ounces) chicken broth
1¼ cups milk
  ½ cup grated Parmesan cheese
  ¼ teaspoon grated nutmeg

1. Place the pumpkin, chicken broth and milk in a medium saucepan. Bring to a simmer over medium-high heat, about 5 minutes.

2. Stir in the cheese and nutmeg and heat through, stirring occasionally, 1 to 2 minutes. Ladle into soup bowls and serve.

4 SERVINGS

PINTO BEAN AND HOMINY SOUP WITH KIELBASA

Our friend Lynette Peters' Croatian grandmother spent half the day making the family's favorite soup—*zrnje*. We made a few convenient substitutions and reduced the cooking time to under 10 minutes. Here is the result; we found it nearly impossible to tell the difference.

2 large garlic cloves
1 can (14½ ounces) beef broth
1 can (15 ounces) pinto beans
1 can (15 ounces) yellow hominy
¼ pound smoked kielbasa

1. Mince the garlic cloves. Place the minced garlic, beef broth and pinto beans with their liquid in a medium saucepan. Drain the hominy and add to the saucepan. Cut the kielbasa into lengthwise quarters, then slice thinly and add to the soup mixture.

2. Bring the soup to a simmer over medium heat, stirring occasionally. Remove about 2 cups of the soup and puree in a food processor or blender. Stir the puree back into the hot soup and serve.

4 SERVINGS

POTATO LEEK SOUP

2 medium leeks
2 tablespoons butter
1 can (1 pound) boiled new potatoes
2 cans (14½ ounces each) chicken broth
½ cup heavy cream

1. Cut a thin slice off the root ends of the leeks and discard. Cut most of the green part off and discard. Cut the leeks in half lengthwise; then slice thinly. Place the leeks in a bowl of cold water. Lift them out into a colander and rinse again under cold water to remove all sand.

2. Melt the butter in a medium saucepan over medium-high heat. Add the leeks and cook, stirring frequently, for 3 to 4 minutes, until the leeks soften.

3. Meanwhile, drain the potatoes. Place the potatoes in a food processor or blender with 1 cup of the chicken broth. Puree until the mixture is fairly smooth. Stir the pureed potatoes and remaining stock into the saucepan with the leeks and cook over medium-high heat until heated through, 1 to 2 minutes. Add the cream and cook, stirring, until well blended and hot, about 30 seconds. Ladle into soup bowls and serve.

4 TO 6 SERVINGS

SPRING PEA SOUP

This lively green soup has all the flavor of freshly picked peas. To save even more time, instead of cooking the bacon as directed in step 1, you can buy precooked bits of real smoked bacon in jars. A nice alternative to the bacon garnish is about ¼ cup chopped fresh mint, which goes especially well with peas.

6 slices of bacon
1 bag (1 pound) frozen peas
2 cans (14½ ounces each) chicken broth

1. Arrange the strips of bacon in a single layer on 4 sheets of microwave-safe paper towels. Cover with 1 more paper towel and microwave on High for 4 minutes and 45 seconds, or until crisp. Let cool slightly, then crumble.

2. While the bacon is cooking, place the peas in a colander and thaw by running hot water over them for about 45 seconds.

3. In a blender or food processor, puree half of the peas at a time with 1 cup of the chicken broth for each batch. Pour the pureed peas into a medium saucepan.

4. Stir in the remaining chicken broth and bring to a simmer over medium-high heat, 3 to 4 minutes, stirring occasionally. Pour the hot soup into bowls, garnish with the bacon bits and serve.

4 SERVINGS

TACO SOUP

Our children named this soup after one of their favorite snacks. You might want to look in your refrigerator for other ingredients to add. Possibilities include: strips of leftover cooked chicken, sliced ripe olives, diced green onions, chopped cilantro and/or a spoonful of hot salsa.

1 can (49½ ounces) chicken broth
1 can (28 ounces) ready-cut peeled tomatoes, diced in juice
1 package (1 pound) frozen corn kernels
3 cups lightly salted tortilla chips (about 3 ounces)
1 package (6 ounces) shredded Monterey Jack cheese
    (1½ cups)

1. In a nonreactive, medium saucepan, combine the chicken broth, the tomatoes and their juices and the corn. Bring to a simmer over medium heat, stirring occasionally, about 5 minutes.

2. Place a handful of tortilla chips in the bottom of 6 to 8 soup plates. Ladle the hot soup over the tortilla chips. Sprinkle some of the shredded cheese over each serving and pass the remaining cheese on the side.

6 TO 8 SERVINGS

TORTELLINI SOUP

It doesn't matter if you buy fresh, frozen or refrigerated tortellini as long as you buy a high-quality brand.

1 can (49½ ounces) chicken broth
1 package (9 ounces) fresh tortellini
¼ pound sliced boiled ham
½ cup loosely packed fresh spinach leaves
½ cup grated Parmesan cheese

1. Pour the chicken broth into a nonreactive, medium saucepan. Bring to a boil over high heat. Add the tortellini and cook according to package directions, until the tortellini are tender but still firm, 6 to 7 minutes.

2. While the tortellini is cooking, cut the ham into thin strips. Place the spinach leaves in a strainer and rinse under cold water. Stack the spinach leaves one on top of the other and slice thinly.

3. Evenly divide the ham and spinach strips among 6 soup plates. Ladle the hot broth and cooked tortellini into the soup plates. Serve with the Parmesan cheese.

6 SERVINGS

3 SALADS

Too many people don't make salads because they say cleaning salad greens takes too long. To save time and trouble, try the procedure that professional cooks use. Fill the sink or a very large bowl with cold water. Separate the leaves of lettuce and add them all at once to the water. Gently swish the leaves through the water. Any sand will drop to the bottom. Then carefully lift out the greens and transfer them to a salad spinner to dry.

There are dozens of fabulous appetizer and main-dish salads you can make in short order. This collection of quick recipes includes a Chicken Salad with Rosemary Mayonnaise; Tuna Salad with Horseradish Mayonnaise; Romaine, Cucumber and Apple Salad; and both a Warm Red Cabbage Salad and a piquant Wilted Spinach Salad that's particularly good with smoked meats or fresh fish.

BASIL TOMATOES WITH WATERCRESS

Serve this salad only when vine-ripened tomatoes and fresh basil are in season. If possible, select both red and yellow tomatoes. If not, use all red tomatoes. Get out your best olive oil to drizzle over them.

1 pint red cherry tomatoes
1 pint yellow pear or plum cherry tomatoes
1 cup loosely packed fresh basil leaves
¼ cup plus 2 tablespoons extra virgin olive oil
    Salt and freshly ground pepper
1 bunch of watercress

1. Rinse the tomatoes. Cut them in half lengthwise and place in a bowl. Wash and dry the basil leaves. Cut the basil into julienne strips and toss with the tomatoes. Drizzle on 2 tablespoons of the olive oil and fold gently to coat the tomatoes lightly. Season with salt and pepper to taste.

2. Break off any large stem ends from the watercress and discard. Rinse the watercress, dry and arrange on 6 salad plates.

3. Spoon the tomato-basil mixture on top of the watercress. Drizzle about ¾ tablespoon of the remaining olive oil over each salad.

6 SERVINGS

BLACK BEAN SALAD OLÉ

Salsa spiked with fresh lime juice makes a great dressing for black beans and sweet corn. Use either kernels cut from fresh corn on the cob or frozen corn kernels that have been thawed but not cooked. This is a good salad for a picnic: It won't wilt no matter how hot it gets outside.

1 can (16 ounces) black beans
1½ cups fresh or frozen corn kernels
½ cup salsa
   Juice of 1 lime
¼ cup chopped fresh cilantro or parsley

1. Drain the black beans. Rinse and drain again. Place in a serving bowl.

2. Add the corn kernels. If using frozen corn, place in a strainer and run briefly under warm water to thaw, then drain well.

3. Fold in the salsa, lime juice and cilantro. Serve immediately or cover and refrigerate until serving time.

4 TO 6 SERVINGS

ITALIAN BREAD SALAD

Whenever you have leftover bread, think of this salad. It's especially good with herbed potato bread.

2 cups large cubes of Italian, French or peasant bread
  (about 1½ inches in diameter)
2 large ripe tomatoes
1 medium red onion
1 cup loosely packed fresh basil leaves
½ cup extra virgin olive oil
  Salt and freshly ground black pepper

1. Toast the cubes of bread under the broiler until golden brown and crunchy. Watch carefully to make sure that the bread doesn't burn.

2. Cut the tomatoes into ¾-inch dice, reserving any juices. Cut the onion into ½-inch dice. Wash the basil leaves and chop coarsely.

3. Place all of the ingredients, including any accumulated tomato juice, into a serving bowl. Pour on the olive oil and toss to coat well. Season to taste with salt and pepper.

6 SERVINGS

INDIAN TOMATO AND CUCUMBER SALAD

While this refreshing salad would be served as a fresh relish in India, I like it as a side salad, especially with grilled chicken or fish. Ground cumin adds a slightly exotic flavor to this colorful melange of ripe tomatoes, red onions and cucumbers.

2 large ripe tomatoes
1 large cucumber
1 small red onion
1 tablespoon sugar
2 teaspoons ground cumin
½ teaspoon salt

1. Cut the tomatoes into ½-inch dice. Peel the cucumber, then quarter lengthwise. With a spoon, scrape out the seeds. Cut the cucumber strips crosswise into ½-inch slices. Peel the red onion and cut into ½-inch dice.

2. Place the vegetables in a serving bowl. Toss to mix. Sprinkle on the sugar, cumin and salt. Stir until all of the vegetables are well seasoned. Serve at room temperature or slightly chilled.

6 TO 8 SERVINGS

APPLE CRUNCH SALAD

Crunchy cubes of apple, jicama, and fennel combine in an interesting salad. Serve it in a salad bowl lined with leaves of curly-edged lettuce.

1 small jicama (1¼ pounds)
1 bulb of fresh fennel
2 tart apples
¾ cup lemon yogurt
2 tablespoons chopped fresh mint or 1 teaspoon dried

1. Peel the jicama and cut into ¾-inch dice. Trim the leaves off the top of the fennel. Trim away the bottom and any wilted outer leaves. Cut the fennel bulb into ¾-inch dice. Core the apples, then cut into ¾-inch dice.

2. Place the jicama, fennel and apples in a serving bowl. Fold in the lemon yogurt and sprinkle with the fresh mint. Serve immediately or cover and chill to serve later. Give a quick stir just before serving.

6 TO 8 SERVINGS

FENNEL, AVOCADO AND BUTTER LETTUCE WITH BALSAMIC VINAIGRETTE

1 bulb of fresh fennel
1 medium-size ripe avocado
2 heads of butter lettuce
⅓ cup extra virgin olive oil
2 tablespoons balsamic vinegar
   Salt and freshly ground pepper

1. Trim the green leaves off the top of the fennel (reserve to use in other recipes). Trim off the bottom and the wilted outer layer. Thinly slice the fennel bulb, then cut the slices into thin strips.

2. Cut the avocado in half. Twist the halves to separate; remove the pit. Peel and cut the avocado into ¾-inch dice.

3. Rinse and dry the butter lettuce leaves. Place them in a salad bowl with the fennel and avocado.

4. Whisk together the oil and vinegar. Season to taste with salt and freshly ground pepper. Pour the dressing over the salad ingredients and toss. Serve immediately.

4 TO 6 SERVINGS

GREEK SALAD

In this tasty salad, ripe cherry tomatoes, cucumbers and feta cheese are deftly dressed with fruity olive oil and oregano. If you have any kalamata or other oil-cured olives, by all means add them, too.

1 pint ripe cherry tomatoes
1 large cucumber
½ pound feta cheese
¼ cup extra virgin olive oil
1 tablespoon dried oregano

1. Remove any stems from the tomatoes. Rinse them, then drain well. Cut the tomatoes in half and place in a serving bowl.

2. Peel the cucumber; quarter lengthwise. With the tip of a spoon, scrape out the seeds. Cut the cucumber crosswise into ½-inch slices. Add the cucumber to the tomatoes in the serving bowl.

3. Crumble the feta cheese over the vegetables. Pour on the olive oil. Sprinkle with the oregano. Toss until well mixed.

6 SERVINGS

JAPANESE LETTUCE SALAD WITH PEANUTS

After years of iceberg lettuce salads as a child, I vowed never to eat it again. Luckily, enough time has passed, and now I can appreciate it for what it is—sweet, juicy, crunchy and an occasional welcome change from the softer, bitter-flavored greens that are currently in vogue.

In this recipe, which was originally given to me by a Japanese friend, the lettuce is dressed with a mild rice wine vinaigrette and garnished with chopped peanuts.

1 small head of iceberg lettuce
¼ cup rice wine vinegar
3 tablespoons vegetable oil
1 tablespoon sugar
¾ cup salted roasted peanuts

1. Cut the head of lettuce in half through the stem. Place the lettuce on a cutting board, cut side-down, and thinly slice to make shreds. Rinse the lettuce, then spin dry. Place the lettuce in a serving bowl.

2. In a small bowl, combine the vinegar, oil and sugar. Stir to dissolve the sugar. Coarsely chop the peanuts in a food processor. Pour the dressing and peanuts over the lettuce and toss until the salad is well mixed. Serve immediately.

4 SERVINGS

MINTED PEA SALAD

This is a nice salad to take to pot lucks and picnics. If it's available, you may want to add diced, cooked bits of pancetta, the Italian bacon, instead of the ham.

1 bag (1 pound) frozen peas
¼ pound slice of cooked smoked ham
½ cup loosely packed fresh mint leaves
½ cup mayonnaise
¼ cup rice wine vinegar

1. Place the frozen peas in a colander and run under warm water to thaw. Cut the ham into ½-inch dice. Chop the fresh mint. Place the peas, ham and mint in a serving bowl.

2. Combine the mayonnaise and rice wine vinegar; stir until well blended. Pour the dressing over the salad and toss until the ingredients are evenly coated. Serve at once or refrigerate to serve later.

4 TO 6 SERVINGS

Moroccan-Style Orange and Radish Salad

Orange flower water, best known as an ingredient in gin fizzes, adds an exotic flavor to this salad. It's available at some supermarkets, liquor stores and pharmacies and in specialty food shops.

4 oranges
8 radishes
2 tablespoons lemon juice
2 teaspoons confectioners' sugar
2 teaspoons orange flower water

1. Peel the oranges and cut them crosswise into ½-inch-thick slices. Arrange the orange slices on a platter. Thinly slice the radishes and spoon them on top of the orange slices.

2. Combine the lemon juice, confectioners' sugar and orange flower water. Sprinkle this dressing over the oranges and radishes and serve.

4 SERVINGS

ROMAINE, CUCUMBER AND APPLE SALAD

This crisp salad is perfect for hot summer days, but it is good all year round, especially since these ingredients are always available. Use lemon cucumbers, if you can find them, for their color, although dark green slicing cucumbers work well, too. Sprinkle toasted sesame seeds on top for a crunchy garnish.

1 small head of romaine lettuce
1 pippin or other flavorful tart apple
1 medium-size cucumber
⅓ cup extra virgin olive oil
2 tablespoons tarragon vinegar

1. Cut the head of romaine in quarters lengthwise; then slice crosswise into 1-inch pieces. Discard the thick core ends. Rinse and dry the lettuce.

2. Core the apple and cut into ½-inch dice. Peel the cucumber, then cut into ½-inch dice. Place the lettuce, apple and cucumber in a salad bowl.

3. Whisk together the oil and vinegar. Pour over the salad and toss gently to coat evenly.

4 TO 6 SERVINGS

SALAD ELIZABETH

Although we've always called this creamy salad dressing Elizabeth dressing, no one remembers who she was. I like to serve it over leaves of young butter lettuce. It's also very nice over melon or mixed fruit salads.

½ cup heavy cream
2 tablespoons lemon juice
1 teaspoon sugar
½ teaspoon grated lemon zest
2 small heads of butter lettuce

1. Combine the cream, lemon juice, sugar and lemon zest. Whisk to blend well. Let stand while you prepare the lettuce.

2. Rinse the leaves of butter lettuce, then dry them. Arrange the lettuce leaves on 4 salad plates. Stir the dressing until smooth. Drizzle the dressing over the greens and serve at once.

4 SERVINGS

SPINACH SALAD WITH MANDARIN ORANGES

Crisp French-fried onion rings and sweet mandarin orange segments turn a basic spinach salad into something special.

1 bag (10 ounces) ready-to-use spinach leaves
1 can (11 ounces) mandarin oranges
½ cup extra virgin olive oil
3 tablespoons balsamic vinegar
1 can (2.8 ounces) French-fried onion rings

1. Rinse the spinach leaves and spin dry. Place them in a salad bowl. Drain the mandarin oranges, reserving the juice, and place the oranges in the bowl.

2. Whisk together the oil, vinegar and 2 tablespoons of reserved orange juice. Pour the dressing over the spinach and toss gently to coat the spinach and oranges.

3. Garnish with the French-fried onion rings and serve.

8 SERVINGS

VEGETABLE CONFETTI SALAD

Here's a great salad to take on picnics or to pot lucks. Make your own vinaigrette or buy a good bottled brand.

1 medium green zucchini
1 medium yellow zucchini or crookneck squash
1 medium carrot
1 sweet red bell pepper
½ cup vinaigrette dressing

1. Using the large holes of a hand grater or the grating disc of a food processor, shred the vegetables.

2. Place them in a bowl and toss with the vinaigrette dressing until well coated. Serve at room temperature or slightly chilled.

4 TO 6 SERVINGS

WARM RED CABBAGE SALAD

If you live near a Chinese market, buy a roast duck for this recipe; otherwise use a barbecued chicken. Many supermarkets sell them in their deli sections. Although this recipe is included in the salad chapter, it's actually filling enough to serve as a light main course.

½ small red cabbage (1 pound)
 1 Chinese roast duck or barbecued chicken
 3 tablespoons vegetable oil
 3 tablespoons balsamic vinegar
 2 tablespoons finely chopped fresh parsley

1. Remove the core from the cabbage. Place the cabbage, cut side down, on a cutting board and slice into thin shreds. Remove the meat from the duck or chicken and cut into strips. Reserve any juices.

2. Heat the oil in a nonreactive, large frying pan. Add the cabbage and cook over high heat, stirring frequently, until the cabbage begins to wilt, 3 to 5 minutes. Pour the vinegar and any accumulated juices from the duck or chicken over the cabbage and toss to coat well. Add the meat and toss.

3. Place the warm cabbage salad on a serving platter. Garnish with the parsley and serve while hot.

4 TO 6 SERVINGS

AVOCADO AND CRABMEAT WITH WATERCRESS MAYONNAISE

Watercress mayonnaise is a tangy dressing for crabmeat and avocado. It's also delicious over baby shrimp stuffed into ripe tomatoes.

1 large ripe avocado
½ pound cooked crabmeat, fresh or canned
½ cup watercress (thick stems removed)
⅓ cup mayonnaise
1 tablespoon lemon juice

1. Cut the avocado in half, remove the pit and scoop out the avocado in one piece to remove the peel. Place an avocado half on each plate. Spoon half the crabmeat over each avocado half.

2. Place the watercress in a blender or food processor. Pulse several times to chop. Add the mayonnaise and lemon juice and process until the dressing is fairly smooth. Spoon some of the dressing over the crabmeat and serve the remainder on the side.

2 SERVINGS

CHICKEN SALAD WITH ROSEMARY MAYONNAISE

It's purported that rosemary strengthens the memory. Although I can't guarantee that this is true, I can promise it will enhance any chicken dish, especially this salad. Serve over mixed greens or use as a sandwich filling.

3 celery ribs
3 cups cubed cooked chicken
⅓ cup mayonnaise
⅓ cup sour cream
1 tablespoon finely chopped fresh rosemary or 1 teaspoon dried rosemary, crumbled

1. Thinly slice the celery and combine in a bowl with the chicken.

2. Blend together the mayonnaise, sour cream and rosemary.

3. Pour the dressing over the chicken and celery. Stir until the ingredients are well coated. Serve immediately, or cover and refrigerate until later.

4 SERVINGS

TUNA SALAD WITH HORSERADISH MAYONNAISE

Horseradish and chopped mint add an interesting zip to turn basic tuna salad into something unusual. Use as a sandwich filling or serve over lettuce.

1 can (12 ounces) tuna
2 celery ribs
½ cup mayonnaise
2 tablespoons chopped fresh mint
2 teaspoons prepared white horseradish

1. Drain the tuna and place it in a mixing bowl. Flake with a fork. Coarsely chop the celery into ½-inch dice. Add the celery to the tuna.

2. Add the mayonnaise, mint and horseradish. Fold into the tuna and celery. Cover and refrigerate if not serving at once.

MAKES 2 CUPS

SMOKED CHICKEN DRESSED WITH PESTO MAYONNAISE

Pesto goes with smoked chicken the way oysters go with Champagne—perfectly!

1½ pounds smoked chicken
½ cup marinated sun-dried tomato halves
1 head of butter lettuce
⅓ cup mayonnaise
3 tablespoons pesto

1. Cut the chicken into 1-inch dice. Cut the tomato halves into thin strips. Separate the head of lettuce into leaves. Rinse and dry the lettuce.

2. Combine the mayonnaise and pesto, stirring until well blended. Then fold in the chicken and tomatoes.

3. Arrange the lettuce leaves on 4 plates. Top with the chicken salad and serve.

4 SERVINGS

WILTED SPINACH SALAD

We like tossing hot dressing over greens and serving the slightly wilted salad under grilled fish. When they are available, we actually prefer to use young mustard greens, instead of spinach, in this recipe.

1 bag (10 ounces) ready-to-use spinach
⅓ cup olive oil
1½ tablespoons soy sauce
1½ tablespoons lemon juice
1½ teaspoons dry mustard

1. Rinse the spinach leaves and dry well.

2. In a large frying pan, whisk together the oil, soy sauce, lemon juice and dry mustard until well blended. Heat over high heat until the mixture is very hot, 1 to 2 minutes. Remove from the heat.

3. Add the spinach leaves to the pan and toss quickly until the spinach is well coated with the dressing and slightly wilted. Immediately remove the salad from the pan so the spinach doesn't cook. Serve at once.

4 SERVINGS

SCALLOP SALAD WITH TARRAGON MAYONNAISE

2 shallots or 4 green onions
3 tablespoons tarragon-flavored vinegar with
    tarragon leaves
1 pound sea scallops
⅓ cup mayonnaise
2 heads of Belgian endive

1. Chop the shallots or finely slice the white part of the green
onion. Place them in a nonreactive frying pan with ¼ cup water
and 1 tablespoon of the vinegar. Bring to a simmer over medium-
high heat. Add the scallops and cook, turning once, just until the
scallops begin to turn white, about 3 minutes. Be careful not to
overcook them. Remove the scallops from the liquid and set
aside. Boil the liquid in the pan over high heat until it's reduced
by half. Remove from the heat.

2. Chop 1 teaspoon of the tarragon leaves from the vinegar and
add to the mayonnaise along with the remaining 2 tablespoons
tarragon vinegar and the reduced cooking liquid. Slice the
scallops thinly and fold them into the dressing.

3. Divide the Belgian endive into individual leaves. Arrange the
leaves on plates and spoon the scallop mixture on top. Serve
slightly warm, at room temperature or chilled.

4 SERVINGS

4 CHICKEN, TURKEY, BEEF, PORK AND LAMB

The limitations of 10 minutes' cooking time and not more than 5 ingredients unleashed a lot of creativity when it came to coming up with recipes for chicken, turkey, pork and lamb chops and beef. Obviously the old standbys—roast chicken and roast pork loin—wouldn't work timewise. We found, however, that by slightly pounding skinless, boneless chicken breast halves to make them a more uniform thickness, they'll cook to perfection in six minutes over high heat (sautéed three minutes per side). Thinly sliced boneless pork loin chops also cook in about six minutes. Thin turkey breast slices are even faster, about two to three minutes. You can even cook a New York strip steak in 10 minutes if you butterfly it first.

With these discoveries, it was a matter of adding lively flavors, such as roasted red pepper strips and capers, or artichoke hearts and green peppercorns, to chicken breasts, or Dijon mustard and whole mustard seeds to pork chops to create some delicious and interesting quick sautés.

CHICKEN BREASTS PICANTE

The trick to preparing this attractive entree in less than 10
minutes is using prepared roasted, peeled red bell peppers. This
recipe is delicious served over quick-cooking rice.

2 tablespoons oil
4 skinless, boneless chicken breast halves (about
   5 ounces each)
1 whole roasted red bell pepper
½ cup dry white wine
1 tablespoon tiny (nonpareil) capers

1. Heat the oil in a large frying pan. Flatten the chicken breasts
slightly. When the oil is hot, add the chicken and cook over high
heat, turning once, until golden brown and white in the center but
still juicy, about 3 minutes on each side.

2. While the chicken is cooking, cut the roasted red pepper into
thin strips.

3. Remove the cooked chicken from the pan. Pour off any excess
oil. Add the wine and bring to a boil over high heat, stirring
constantly to loosen any browned bits on the bottom of the pan.
Add the red pepper strips. Stir in the capers without draining
them, so that some of the vinegar in which they were packed is
included. Spoon the sauce over the chicken and serve.

4 SERVINGS

BROILED CHICKEN WITH TEQUILA AND LIME

On a day when you have more than 10 minutes, you might want to try this sweet tequila lime basting sauce on flank steak.

4 skinless, boneless chicken breast halves
   (about 5 ounces each)
⅓ cup tequila
2 tablespoons honey
   Grated zest and juice from 1 lime
½ teaspoon ground cumin

1. Preheat the broiler. Pound the chicken breasts slightly to flatten evenly.

2. In a medium bowl, combine the tequila, honey, lime zest and juice and ground cumin. Stir to mix well. Add the chicken pieces and turn several times until the chicken is well coated with the marinade.

3. Place the chicken breasts on a broiler pan. Broil about 4 inches from the heat, turning once and basting several times with the sauce for the first 5 minutes, until the chicken is browned outside and white to the center, 6 to 8 minutes total.

4 SERVINGS

APRICOT-SAUCED CHICKEN

Rice or couscous alongside will ensure that none of this tasty sauce is lost. You can use fresh apricots when they are in season. Add them to the pan along with the wine at the start of step 2.

4 skinless, boneless chicken breast halves
  (about 5 ounces each)
  Salt and freshly ground pepper
2 tablespoons vegetable oil
¼ cup dry white wine
½ cup heavy cream
12 canned apricot halves (8½-ounce can)

1. Pound the chicken breasts slightly to flatten evenly. Season lightly with salt and pepper. Heat the oil in a large frying pan. add the chicken breasts and cook over high heat for 3 minutes. Turn the chicken over and cook for 3 minutes longer, or until white throughout but still moist. Remove the chicken breasts to a platter.

2. Pour off any excess fat from the frying pan. Add the wine to the pan and boil over high heat until reduced by half, about 1 minute. Pour in the cream and boil until slightly reduced and thickened, about 2 minutes. Season the sauce with salt and pepper to taste. Add the apricots and warm through. Pour the sauce and apricots over the chicken on the platter and serve.

4 SERVINGS

BREAST OF CHICKEN IN SWEET RED PEPPER SAUCE

One of the most versatile convenience foods in markets today is sweet red bell peppers, which you can buy already roasted and peeled and packed in jars. These tasty peppers lend a sweet flavor to numerous dishes—everything from a quick ratatouille to this creamy, fresh-tasting sauce.

4 skinless, boneless chicken breast halves
   (about 5 ounces each)
2 tablespoons oil
3 whole roasted red bell peppers
1½ tablespoons heavy cream or milk
1 teaspoon dried Italian herb seasoning or fines herbes

1. Flatten the chicken breasts slightly. Heat the oil in a large frying pan. When the oil is hot, add the chicken breasts and cook over high heat for about 3 minutes on each side, until golden brown outside and white in the center but still moist.

2. While the chicken is cooking, place the peppers in a blender or food processor. Add the cream and herbs and puree until the sauce is smooth. If desired, warm the sauce in a microwave for about 45 seconds on High. Spoon the sauce over the chicken and serve.

4 SERVINGS

CARIBBEAN CHICKEN CURRY

We often serve this flavorful curried chicken over the Coconut Raisin Rice on page 156. If you like, provide a selection of garnishes, such as chopped green pepper, tomatoes, cucumber, pineapple and roasted peanuts. Let your guests sprinkle on what they like.

1½ pounds skinless, boneless chicken breasts and/or thighs
   3 tablespoons oil
   3 tablespoons good-quality curry powder, preferably
      Madras style
   1 cup unsweetened coconut milk
¼ teaspoon salt
   2 tablespoons lime juice

1. Cut chicken into 2-inch pieces. Heat the oil in a large frying pan. Add the chicken pieces and season with the curry powder. Cook over high heat, stirring occasionally, until the chicken begins to brown, about 4 minutes.

2. Reduce the temperature to medium and stir in the coconut milk. Cook, stirring occasionally, until the sauce begins to thicken slightly, about 4 minutes longer. Season with the salt. Then stir in the lime juice. Cook for 1 minute longer, then serve.

4 SERVINGS

CHEESY CHICKEN

Everyone loves this recipe for mustard-flavored chicken breasts baked under a blanket of cheese and bread crumbs.

6 skinless, boneless chicken breast halves
  (about 5 ounces each)
⅓ cup Dijon mustard
¼ cup dry white wine
2 cups fresh bread crumbs
1 cup grated Romano cheese

1. Heat the oven to 500 degrees F. Pound the chicken breasts to flatten slightly. Combine the mustard and wine in a shallow dish; stir to blend. In another shallow dish, combine the bread crumbs and cheese; toss to mix. Lightly coat a baking sheet with nonstick vegetable spray.

2. Dip the chicken into the mustard mixture, turning to coat both sides. Then dredge the chicken in the crumbs to coat well. Place the chicken on the baking sheet. Repeat the steps to coat the remaining chicken breasts.

3. Bake for about 8 minutes, until the chicken is white in the center but still juicy and the crumb coating is golden brown. If the crumbs aren't brown enough, place under the broiler for another minute or so.

6 SERVINGS

CHICKEN AND ARTICHOKE HEARTS WITH GREEN PEPPERCORNS

Green peppercorns add a nice peppery flavor to this rustic dish.

1 package (10 ounces) frozen artichoke hearts
4 skinless, boneless chicken breast halves
   (about 5 ounces each)
¼ teaspoon salt
2 tablespoons olive oil
1 tablespoon green peppercorns in brine
1 teaspoon dried thyme leaves

1. Run artichokes under hot water and break them apart, or microwave on High for 1 to 2 minutes, until you can separate them.

2. Gently pound the chicken to flatten slightly. Season the chicken with salt. Heat the oil in a large frying pan. Add the chicken breasts and cook over high heat for 3 minutes.

3. Turn the chicken over and add the artichoke hearts. Cover and continue cooking for 3 minutes. Then uncover, add the green peppercorns and thyme and cook for 2 minutes longer.

4. Remove the chicken breasts to a serving platter. Pour the artichokes and peppercorns over and serve.

4 SERVINGS

QUICK CHICKEN PAPRIKASH

It's worth buying full-flavored imported sweet Hungarian paprika for this recipe. Serve over quick-cooking rice or fresh pasta.

1½ pounds skinless, boneless chicken breasts or cut-up
    boneless chicken pieces
1 medium onion
2 tablespoons oil
1 cup sour cream
2 tablespoons paprika
    Salt and freshly ground pepper

1. Cut the chicken crosswise into strips about ½-inch wide. Thinly slice the onion.

2. Heat the oil in a large frying pan. Add the onion. Cook over medium-high heat, stirring occasionally, until the onion is translucent, about 3 minutes. Push to one side. Add the chicken strips and cook, stirring, until the chicken begins to brown, about 3 minutes longer.

3. Reduce the heat to medium. Combine the sour cream and paprika. Stir into the chicken and onion mixture. Season with salt and pepper to taste. Heat through without allowing the sauce to boil. Serve immediately.

4 SERVINGS

CHICKEN WITH BRAISED LETTUCE AND CHERRY TOMATOES

The first time my husband cooked dinner for me, he surprised me by cooking the salad! The whole meal was ready in less than 10 minutes.

4 skinless, boneless chicken breast halves
  (about 5 ounces each)
  Salt and freshly ground pepper
1 head of romaine lettuce
6 tablespoons butter
1 tablespoon dried fines herbes or herbes de Provence
1 pint cherry tomatoes

1. Preheat the oven to 400 degrees F. Gently pound the chicken breasts to flatten slightly. Season with salt and pepper to taste.

2. Trim the root end off the head of romaine. Then cut off the top third (reserve to serve for salad another time), leaving a lettuce that's about 7 inches long. Cut the lettuce lengthwise into quarters and rinse under cold running water.

3. Melt the butter in a large frying pan over high heat, swirling to avoid browning the butter. Place the lettuce wedges in an 8-by-11-inch baking dish. Pour 4 tablespoons of the melted butter over the lettuce and bake for 5 to 6 minutes, until the lettuce is hot and wilted.

4. Meanwhile, place the chicken in the butter remaining in the frying pan. Season with half the herbs and cook over high heat, turning once, for 3 minutes per side, until browned outside and white but still juicy in the center. Remove the chicken to a platter. Add the cherry tomatoes to the frying pan. Season them with the remaining herbs and cook over high heat, stirring, until heated through, about 1 minute. Arrange the lettuce and tomatoes around the chicken and serve.

4 SERVINGS

BREAST OF CHICKEN WITH LEMON BUTTER

Serve this tangy lemon chicken with herbed vermicelli for a quick company meal. By dipping the chicken first in the flour and then in the egg—it's usually the other way around—the coating comes out more like a batter.

2 lemons
¼ cup flour
   Salt and freshly ground pepper
4 skinless, boneless chicken breast halves
   (about 5 ounces each)
1 egg, beaten with 2 tablespoons water
4 tablespoons butter

1. Peel 1 lemon. Cut the fruit into thin slices. Remove and discard any seeds. Squeeze the other lemon and set the juice aside. Season the flour with salt and pepper to taste.

2. Pound the chicken breasts to flatten slightly. Dip the chicken in the flour, lightly coating both sides; then dip in the beaten egg mixed with water.

3. Melt half the butter in a large frying pan over medium-high heat. When the butter is sizzling, add the chicken and cook until golden brown on one side, about 3 minutes. Turn over and cook until brown on the second side and white but still moist in the center, about 3 minutes longer. Place the chicken on a serving platter. Cover with aluminum foil to keep warm.

4. Add the remaining 2 tablespoons butter to the hot pan. Stir in the lemon juice. Quickly heat through, stirring to loosen any browned bits. Pour the sauce over the chicken. Garnish with the lemon slices and serve.

4 SERVINGS

SMOKED CHICKEN WITH BLACK-EYED PEAS AND RASPBERRY SAUCE

The juices from the smoked chicken add wonderful flavor to the black-eyed peas in this recipe, and the tart-sweet raspberries provide a lovely counterpoint to the smokiness of the meat. Here's a company meal that you can leisurely put on the table in less than 10 minutes. The Wilted Spinach Salad on page 65 is a nice accompaniment.

2 cans (15 ounces each) black-eyed peas
1 whole smoked chicken (about 3 to 3½ pounds)
1 package (10 ounces) frozen raspberries
¼ cup port

1. Drain the black-eyed peas. Rinse and drain again. Place the peas in a shallow 3- to 4-quart microwave-safe casserole.

2. Cut the chicken into serving pieces and arrange them on top of the peas. Place in the microwave and cook on Medium-High (80 percent power) for about 5 minutes, until the peas and chicken are heated through.

3. Meanwhile, place the raspberries in a small saucepan. Add the port and heat gently, stirring occasionally. To serve, spoon the warm raspberry sauce over the chicken. Pass any extra sauce on the side.

4 TO 6 SERVINGS

TURKEY À LA PARMIGIANA

Meat markets today offer a large selection of turkey cuts. We find the boneless turkey breast slices perfect for fast feasts. This dinner is ready in minutes. Serve it with fresh pasta tossed with garlic butter.

1 pound boneless turkey breast slices
Salt and freshly ground pepper
½ cup prepared marinara sauce or extra-chunky spaghetti
sauce with crushed garlic
1 package (8 ounces) sliced Monterey Jack cheese
½ cup grated Parmesan cheese

1. Preheat the broiler. Season the turkey slices with salt and pepper to taste. Arrange the turkey slices on a broiler pan and broil 3 to 4 inches from the heat just until the turkey begins to turn opaque, about 2 to 3 minutes.

2. Remove the turkey from the oven and spread some of the sauce over each slice. Then cover with a slice of cheese. Sprinkle the Parmesan on top and return to the broiler until the cheese is melted, 1 to 2 minutes. Serve immediately.

3 TO 4 SERVINGS

TURKEY TONNATO

Substituting boneless turkey breast slices for veal roast allows you to make this variation on vitello tonnato, the classic veal dish, in less than 10 minutes. It's especially nice to serve during warm weather.

1 pound thinly sliced boneless turkey breast
1 can (about 6⅛ ounces) tuna packed in water
⅓ cup milk
3 tablespoons mayonnaise
3 tablespoons tiny (nonpareil) capers

1. Arrange the turkey slices on a broiler pan in a single layer. Broil 3 to 4 inches from the heat, turning once, until the turkey is white throughout, about 4 minutes.

2. Drain the tuna and place it in a bowl. Flake with a fork. Stir in the milk, mayonnaise and capers until well blended.

3. When the turkey is done, arrange the slices on a serving platter and spoon the tuna sauce over each slice.

4 SERVINGS

TURKEY WITH PROSCIUTTO AND MUSHROOMS

A little bit of prosciutto goes a long way to season mild turkey breast slices. Serve this festive dish over rice or thin egg noodles.

½ pound fresh mushrooms
1 pound thinly sliced boneless turkey breast
   Salt and freshly ground pepper
2 tablespoons olive oil
¼ pound thinly sliced prosciutto
¼ cup dry vermouth

1. Slice the mushrooms. Season the turkey slices with salt and pepper to taste. Heat the oil in a large frying pan. Add the turkey slices and cook over high heat, turning once, until the turkey is white throughout, 3 to 4 minutes. Remove the turkey to a platter.

2. Add the mushrooms and prosciutto to the frying pan and cook, stirring, until the mushrooms begin to brown, about 4 minutes. Return the turkey slices to the pan and spoon the prosciutto and mushrooms over them. Add the vermouth and heat through, about 15 seconds. Serve immediately.

3 TO 4 SERVINGS

SKILLET BEEF STEW IN RED WINE

Frozen peas and pearl onions need only to be heated through. If you have any leftover cooked vegetables, such as carrots or potatoes, feel free to add them, too.

 1 package (10 ounces) frozen peas and pearl onions
1½ pounds boneless beef tenderloin tips
 2 tablespoons oil
 ½ cup dry red wine
 1 teaspoon dried thyme leaves
 Salt and freshly ground pepper

1. Run frozen vegetables under hot water or microwave on High for 1 to 2 minutes to thaw. Drain well.

2. Cut the beef into 1-inch cubes. Heat the oil in a large frying pan. Add the beef cubes and cook over high heat, stirring, until the beef is browned on all sides, about 4 minutes.

3. Add the wine and thyme. Cook for 2 minutes. Then stir in the peas and pearl onions and continue cooking, stirring occasionally, until the vegetables are heated through, about 2 minutes longer. Season to taste with salt and pepper and serve.

4 SERVINGS

STREAMLINED STROGANOFF

The less expensive tenderloin tails of beef are perfect for this recipe. You may want to save even more time by asking the butcher to cut the meat into strips for stroganoff for you. Chicken or turkey pieces can also be used. Stroganoff is delicious served over egg noodles.

1 pound boneless beef tenderloin tips
¾ pound mushrooms
2 tablespoons oil
½ cup sour cream
2 tablespoons ketchup
Salt and freshly ground pepper

1. Cut the beef into ½-inch-thick slices. Then cut the slices of meat into thin strips about ½ inch wide. Cut the mushrooms into thin slices.

2. Heat the oil in a large frying pan. Add the meat and cook over high heat, stirring, until the meat is browned all over, about 3 minutes.

3. Add the mushrooms and continue to cook, stirring, until the mushrooms begin to release their moisture, about 3 minutes. Stir in the sour cream and ketchup and heat through. Season to taste with salt and pepper and serve.

3 TO 4 SERVINGS

MUSTARD-SAUCED PORK CHOPS

A splash of red wine stirred in at the end of the cooking makes an instant sauce for these succulent pork chops.

4 boneless center-cut pork chops (about 5 ounces each)
4 teaspoons Dijon mustard
½ cup plus 2 tablespoons yellow mustard seeds
2 tablespoons olive oil
½ cup dry red wine

1. Lightly pound the pork chops until they are about ½ inch thick. Spread the mustard lightly over the chops. Sprinkle with the mustard seeds to coat. Turn the meat over and cover the other side with the mustard and mustard seeds.

2. Heat the oil in a frying pan large enough to hold the chops in a single layer. Add the pork chops and cook over medium-high heat, turning once, until nicely browned outside with no trace of pink in the center, about 3 minutes on each side. Remove the meat to a platter and cover with foil to keep warm.

3. Pour the wine into the pan and bring to a boil over medium-high heat, scraping loose any browned bits from the bottom of the pan and any mustard seeds that didn't cling to the meat. Boil, stirring, until the sauce is slightly reduced, 1 to 2 minutes. Pour the sauce over the chops and serve.

4 SERVINGS

PORK MEDALLIONS WITH APRICOT GLAZE

This is an easy company dinner. Serve the glazed pork over orzo, the rice-shaped pasta.

1½ pork tenderloins (about 1 pound)
    Salt and freshly ground pepper
  1 small garlic clove
  2 tablespoons vegetable oil
  ¼ cup port
  2 tablespoons apricot jam

1. Cut the pork tenderloins into 8 medallions about ¾ inch thick. Season with salt and pepper. Mince the garlic. Heat the oil in a large frying pan over high heat. When the oil is hot, add the pork medallions and cook, turning once, until the pork is nicely browned outside with no trace of pink in the center, about 6 minutes total cooking time. Remove the pork to a platter.

2. Add the garlic to the pan and cook, stirring, for 30 seconds. Whisk in the port and apricot jam and boil over high heat, stirring, another minute or so. Return the pork and any accumulated juices to the pan and heat through. Serve immediately.

3 TO 4 SERVINGS

PORK ADOBO

For a traditional adobo, the pork is slowly braised in a sauce of vinegar, soy sauce and garlic. With one eye on the clock, we found we could get the same flavor in a fraction of the time. This recipe works well with boneless chicken breasts or turkey, too.

4 boneless center-cut pork chops (about 4 ounces each)
3 large garlic cloves
½ cup plus 1 tablespoon distilled white vinegar
3 tablespoons soy sauce
1 teaspoon cornstarch

1. Lightly pound the pork chops until they're about ½ inch thick. Mince the garlic.

2. In a nonreactive, medium frying pan, combine the garlic, ½ cup of the vinegar and the soy sauce. Bring to a simmer over high heat. Add the pork and cook, turning once, until the pork is cooked through with no trace of pink in the center, about 5 minutes. Remove the pork to a serving platter.

3. Dissolve the cornstarch in 1 tablespoon of the vinegar. Whisk the dissolved cornstarch into the hot sauce. Cook, whisking continually, until the sauce thickens, about 1 minute. Pour the sauce over the meat and serve.

4 SERVINGS

LAMB CHOPS À LA GRECQUE

Lemon juice, oregano and garlic—favorite flavors of Greece—do wonders for lamb chops.

4 loin or rib lamb chops (1 inch thick)
½ teaspoon salt
¼ teaspoon freshly ground pepper
2 garlic cloves
2 tablespoons lemon juice
1 tablespoon dried oregano leaves

1. Preheat the broiler. Season the lamb chops on both sides with the salt and pepper. Place them on a broiler pan. Crush the garlic through a press into a small bowl. Stir in the lemon juice and oregano. Place a spoonful of the lemon-garlic mixture on top of each lamb chop. Smear to coat. Turn them over and top the second side with the remaining lemon garlic mixture.

2. Place the chops under the broiler 3 to 4 inches from the heat and broil until done, about 3 to 4 minutes per side for medium rare.

2 SERVINGS

A SPECIAL JOE

This is a simplified version of Joe's Special, a San Francisco scrambled egg tradition.

1 package (10 ounces) frozen chopped spinach
1 medium onion
1 pound ground beef
8 eggs
  Salt and freshly ground pepper
4 kaiser rolls, split in half

1. Put the spinach in a microwave-safe dish. Microwave on High until thawed, about 2 minutes. Drain off excess moisture.

2. Cut the onion into quarters and place in a food processor. Pulse several times to chop the onion.

3. In a large frying pan, cook the meat and chopped onion over high heat, stirring occasionally, until the meat is no longer pink, about 3 minutes. Stir in the spinach.

4. Beat the eggs until frothy. Season well with salt and pepper. Add the eggs to the frying pan. Cook, stirring, until the eggs are set, about 3 to 4 minutes. Serve over the sliced rolls.

4 TO 6 SERVINGS

BUTTERFLIED STEAKS WITH SUN-DRIED TOMATOES AND MUSHROOMS

To save time, ask your butcher to butterfly the steaks. Or do it yourself by cutting each in half horizontally almost to the edge, then opening up the steak like a book.

2 New York strip steaks (about 8 ounces each)
2 shallots
¼ pound mushrooms
¼ cup marinated sun-dried tomatoes plus
    2 tablespoons of the oil
¼ cup beef broth

1. Butterfly the steaks and pound them slightly to flatten evenly. Mince the shallots. Thinly slice the mushrooms.

2. Heat the oil from the tomatoes in a large frying pan. Add the steaks and cook over high heat, turning once, until brown on both sides, about 3 minutes per side for medium rare. Be careful you don't overcook the meat. Once the steaks are brown on both sides, remove them to a platter. Cover with foil to keep warm.

3. Add the shallots, mushrooms and sun-dried tomatoes to the frying pan. Cook over high heat, stirring frequently, until the mushrooms begin to soften, about 3 minutes. Stir in the broth and boil for 1 minute. Pour the sauce over the steaks and serve.

2 SERVINGS

MOROCCAN LAMB KEBABS

Serve these tasty lamb kebabs with quick-cooking couscous. Diced cucumber mixed with plain yogurt is a nice accompaniment. If you have time, it's a good idea to soak the wooden skewers for 15 minutes in a bowl of cold water so they don't char.

½ small onion
¼ cup loosely packed mint leaves
1 teaspoon cinnamon
¼ teaspoon salt
¼ teaspoon freshly ground pepper
1 pound lean ground lamb

1. Preheat the broiler. Chop the onion and mint leaves. Add the onion, chopped mint, cinnamon, salt and pepper to the lamb. Stir gently until well combined.

2. Divide the seasoned lamb into 8 equal parts. Roll each part into a cylindrical shape about 4 inches long. Push a wooden skewer lengthwise through each meat cylinder.

3. Cook the meat under the broiler about 4 inches from the heat, turning occasionally, until browned outside and only barely pink in the center, about 6 minutes.

3 TO 4 SERVINGS

5 FISH AND SHELLFISH

Cooking fish and shellfish in 10 minutes or less is easy, because fish is tender to begin with and only has to be heated through. The challenge is not to overcook it and thus dry it out.

In general, we go along with the Canadian Fisheries cooking theory that estimates 10 minutes' cooking time for every inch of thickness measured at the thickest part of the fish. Shrimp, on the other hand, are done as soon as they turn bright pink and curl. Scallops are cooked to their succulent best when they turn snowy white.

Garlic, anchovies, capers, lemon zest, mustard, ginger and other assertive seasonings are all great enhancements for fish. The recipes in this chapter range from crispy Quick Salmon Croquettes served with Lemon-Caper Mayonnaise to Sautéed Catfish Fillets topped with a spicy Pecan Brown Butter Sauce.

In most of the following recipes, one similar fish variety is interchangeable with another. It's always best to go to the market with an open mind. Find a fishmonger you trust and then take his or her advice on the freshest catch of the day.

PAN-FRIED CATFISH WITH PECAN PARSLEY SAUCE

Reserve a few pecan halves to sprinkle on top as a garnish. This flavorful green sauce is also delicious over fried perch or rockfish.

    4 catfish fillets (about 6 ounces each)
        Salt and freshly ground pepper
    ½ cup plus 2 tablespoons extra virgin olive oil
    1 cup pecan halves
    1 cup loosely packed parsley
    ¼ cup grated Parmesan cheese

1. Season the fish fillets with salt and pepper to taste. Heat 2 tablespoons of the olive oil in a large frying pan. Add the catfish and cook, turning once, for 2 to 3 minutes per side, or until the fish flakes easily.

2. While the fish is cooking, place the remaining ½ cup olive oil in a food processor or blender along with ¾ cup of the pecans, the parsley and the Parmesan cheese. Puree until fairly smooth.

3. To serve, spoon 1 to 2 tablespoons of the green sauce over each fish fillet. Garnish each with 1 tablespoon of the remaining pecan halves. Any extra sauce can be kept in the refrigerator for at least a week or in the freezer for several months.

4 SERVINGS

SAUTÉED CATFISH FILLETS WITH PECAN BROWN BUTTER SAUCE

Cayenne pepper adds a spicy edge to the brown butter and toasted pecan sauce in this recipe.

½ cup flour
  Salt and freshly ground pepper
 4 catfish fillets (about 6 ounces each)
 4 tablespoons butter
 1 cup pecan halves
 ¼ teaspoon cayenne pepper

1. Place flour on a plate. Season flour generously with salt and pepper. Lightly coat both sides of the fish fillets with the seasoned flour.

2. Melt 2 tablespoons of the butter in a large frying pan over medium-high heat. Add the fish and cook, turning once, until the fish is golden brown on both sides and flakes easily, about 2 to 3 minutes per side. Transfer the fish to a serving platter.

3. Add the remaining 2 tablespoons butter to the frying pan along with the pecans and cayenne. Cook over medium-high heat, stirring, until the butter turns golden brown and the nuts are toasted, 2 to 3 minutes; do not burn. Pour the sauce over the fish and serve.

4 SERVINGS

COD WRAPPED IN LETTUCE LEAVES

A Pernod-orange butter bastes this attractive fish, lending it the lightest flavor of licorice.

1½ pounds cod fillet
    Salt and freshly ground pepper
 ⅓ cup Pernod
  4 large leaves of butter lettuce
  4 tablespoons butter
 ¼ cup undiluted orange juice concentrate

1. Preheat the broiler. Cut the cod into 4 equal pieces. Season with salt and pepper to taste. Spoon ½ tablespoon of the Pernod over each fish fillet. Wrap each piece of cod in a lettuce leaf, folding up the sides as if you were wrapping a package. Place the fish, seam-side down, in a flameproof baking dish or gratin.

2. Cut up the butter into a small glass bowl. Microwave on High for 30 to 60 seconds, until melted. Stir the orange juice concentrate and the remaining Pernod into the melted butter.

3. Broil the fish about 4 inches from the heat, basting several times with the butter sauce to keep the lettuce moist, for 8 minutes without turning. Transfer to plates, pour the pan juices and any butter sauce remaining in the bowl over the packets and serve.

4 SERVINGS

BROILED HALIBUT WITH ANCHOVY LEMON BUTTER

Remembering the recipe for this butter sauce is as easy as three, two, one!

4 halibut steaks or fillets (about 6 ounces each)
 Salt and freshly ground pepper
3 tablespoons butter
2 tablespoons lemon juice
1 tablespoon anchovy paste or finely chopped anchovies

1. Preheat the broiler. Season the halibut steaks with salt and pepper. Place on a broiler pan and broil about 4 inches from the heat, turning once, until opaque throughout, about 5 minutes.

2. Melt the butter in a small saucepan over medium-low heat. Whisk in the lemon juice and anchovy paste until well blended. Spoon the sauce over the halibut and serve.

4 SERVINGS

SALMON FILLETS WITH SAUTÉED CUCUMBERS

It's a shame that cucumbers are almost always served cold. Sautéing them quickly in a little butter makes them exceptionally sweet and a wonderful accompaniment for fish.

4 salmon fillets (6 to 8 ounces each)
  Salt and freshly ground pepper
2 medium cucumbers
3 tablespoons butter
1 tablespoon chopped fresh dill or 1 teaspoon dried

1. Season the salmon fillets with salt and pepper to taste. Place them on a broiler pan. Preheat the broiler.

2. Peel the cucumbers. Quarter them lengthwise. With the tip of a spoon, scrape out the seeds. Cut crosswise into ¾-inch dice.

3. Place the salmon under the broiler about 4 inches from the heat. Broil until just opaque in the center, 5 to 7 minutes.

4. Meanwhile, melt the butter in a large frying pan over medium-high heat. Add the cucumbers and dill and cook, stirring, until the cucumbers are heated through, 1 to 2 minutes. Season with salt and pepper to taste. Serve the cucumbers with the salmon.

4 SERVINGS

SALMON PAILLARDS WITH ORANGE-CHILI BUTTER

Paillards are very thin slices of salmon that weigh about 2 ounces each and cook in about a minute. Ask your fishmonger to slice the salmon for you.

4 ounces (½ container) whipped butter
¼ cup undiluted orange juice concentrate
1½ teaspoons chili powder
½ teaspoon grated orange zest
8 thin slices of salmon fillet (each piece should weigh about 2 ounces and be about ¼ inch thick)
Salt and freshly ground pepper

1. Preheat the broiler. If the butter isn't very soft, place in a glass or ceramic bowl and microwave on High for 10 seconds. Beat in the orange juice concentrate, chili powder and orange zest.

2. With your hands, gently press each salmon fillet to flatten slightly. Place the salmon paillards on a large baking sheet. Season with salt and pepper to taste.

3. Broil the salmon paillards about 4 inches from the heat until the fish turns pink and opaque, about 2 minutes. Remove to serving plates and top with a spoonful of the orange-chili butter. Serve immediately.

4 SERVINGS

QUICK SALMON CROQUETTES

This easy, crispy version of the old-fashioned favorite can be served simply with a lemon wedge for squeezing over the top or dressed up with the Lemon-Caper Mayonnaise that follows.

1 can (15½ ounces) salmon
2 green onions
½ cup dry seasoned bread crumbs
1 egg
   Vegetable oil

1. Drain the salmon, place in a bowl and flake with a fork. Thinly slice the green onions and add them to the salmon along with 2 tablespoons of the bread crumbs and the egg. Mix to blend well.

2. Form into 6 oval patties ½ to ¾ inch thick. Dip the patties in the remaining bread crumbs to coat.

3. Heat about ¼ inch of oil in a large skillet over medium heat. Add the salmon patties and cook, turning once, until both sides are crisp and golden and the croquettes are heated through, about 7 minutes total.

3 SERVINGS (2 CROQUETTES EACH)

LEMON-CAPER MAYONNAISE

½ cup mayonnaise
2 tablespoons fresh lemon juice
1 tablespoon tiny (nonpareil) capers or chopped
   large capers
1 tablespoon chopped fresh dill or ½ teaspoon dried
   Dash of cayenne pepper

In a small bowl, combine all the ingredients. Stir to blend well.
Cover and refrigerate until serving time.

MAKES ABOUT ⅔ CUP

BROILED SCALLOPS WITH GARLIC BREAD CRUMBS

1 pound sea scallops
4 tablespoons butter
1 garlic clove
1 cup fresh bread crumbs
2 tablespoons finely chopped fresh parsley

1. Preheat the broiler. If the scallops are larger than 1 inch, slice them in half crosswise. Thread scallops on 4 thin metal skewers.

2. Cut the butter into ½-inch pieces and place in a microwave-safe pie plate. Microwave on High for 30 to 60 seconds, until the butter is melted. Crush the garlic through a press and stir it into the butter.

3. Place the bread crumbs on a plate. Add the parsley and toss to mix.

4. Roll the scallops in the garlic butter, turning to coat all sides. Then roll them in the bread crumbs.

5. Arrange the skewers on a broiler pan. Broil about 4 inches from the heat, turning once, until done to your taste, 3 to 5 minutes. Serve immediately.

4 SERVINGS

SCALLOPS WITH GINGER AND GRAPEFRUIT SAUCE

Fresh grapefruit juice makes all the difference in this easy scallop dish. Serve the pan juices over cooked rice or orzo (tiny rice-shaped pasta) and accompany the fish with crisp sugar snap peas.

¼ cup grapefruit juice
¼ cup Riesling or other fruity white wine
1½ teaspoons ground ginger
3 tablespoons butter
1 pound bay scallops

1. In a small bowl, combine the grapefruit juice, wine and ginger. Whisk briskly to dissolve the ginger.

2. Melt the butter in a large frying pan over high heat. Add the scallops and cook, stirring frequently, until the scallops are opaque in the center, 2 to 3 minutes. Remove the scallops with a slotted spoon and place on a serving platter.

3. Add the grapefruit juice mixture to the pan. Bring to a boil over high heat and cook, whisking, until the sauce is slightly reduced, 1 to 2 minutes. Return the scallops to the pan and cook, stirring, until heated through, about 30 seconds. Serve immediately.

4 SERVINGS

BROILED TUNA WITH AN ORANGE SESAME GLAZE

When tuna isn't available, this marinade can be used with any flavorful fish, such as swordfish, pollack, cod or halibut.

½ cup orange juice
1 tablespoon plus 1 teaspoon soy sauce
1 teaspoon Asian sesame oil
½ teaspoon grated fresh ginger or powdered ginger
4 fresh tuna steaks (6 to 8 ounces each)

1. In a 1-quart resealable plastic bag, combine the orange juice, soy sauce, sesame oil and ginger. (If you use powdered ginger, dissolve it in the soy sauce before combining with the other ingredients.) Add the tuna steaks and let them marinate for 5 minutes. Or, place the marinade and fish in a shallow pan. Turn the fish frequently while it's marinating.

2. Preheat the broiler. Remove the tuna steaks from the marinade and arrange on a broiler pan; reserve the marinade. Broil 3 to 4 inches from the heat for 4 to 5 minutes, turning the steaks over once, until the fish is just opaque throughout but still juicy.

3. Meanwhile, pour the marinade into a small saucepan and boil over medium-high heat until reduced to about ¼ cup, 1 to 2 minutes. To serve, spoon the glaze over the fish.

4 SERVINGS

SEA BASS COOKED IN RED WINE

Cooking fish in red wine isn't as odd as it may seem; many classic French recipes do just that. In this dish, a full-flavored wine, such as a Merlot, will complement the garlic-scented sea bass nicely.

4 sea bass fillets (5 to 6 ounces each)
Salt and freshly ground pepper
1½ teaspoons herbes de Provence
3 large garlic cloves
2 tablespoons extra virgin olive oil
⅓ cup dry red wine

1. Season the sea bass fillets with salt and pepper to taste. Sprinkle the herbes de Provence over both sides of the fish.

2. Mince the garlic. Heat the olive oil in a large frying pan. Add the garlic and cook over medium heat, stirring, until softened and fragrant, about 1 minute.

3. Add the sea bass to the pan and cook, turning once, until the fish flakes easily, about 5 minutes total. Transfer the fish fillets to a platter or individual plates.

4. Add the red wine to the frying pan. Boil over high heat, stirring, until reduced to about ¼ cup, 1 to 2 minutes. Spoon the sauce over the fish and serve.

4 SERVINGS

SPICY GARLIC SHRIMP

If you're very bold, add another half teaspoon of hot red pepper flakes. Be sure to serve crusty bread to soak up all of the garlicky juices.

    4 large garlic cloves
1½ pounds shelled and deveined medium-large shrimp
       (20 to 25 per pound)
¼ cup olive oil
½ teaspoon dried hot red pepper flakes
⅓ cup dry white wine
½ teaspoon salt

1. Mince the garlic cloves and combine in a medium bowl with the shrimp, olive oil and hot pepper flakes. Stir to coat the shrimp with the oil and seasonings. Marinate 5 minutes.

2. Heat a large heavy frying pan over medium-high heat. When the pan is hot, add the shrimp and seasoned oil. Spread out the shrimp in a single layer. When the shrimp turn pink on the bottom, about 2 minutes, turn them over and continue cooking just until they are done, 1 to 2 minutes longer. Remove the shrimp from the pan and place in a serving bowl.

3. Add the wine and salt to the frying pan. Bring to a boil, stirring. Pour over the shrimp and serve at once.

4 SERVINGS

SHRIMP IN GARLIC CREAM SAUCE

If you let the fishmonger shell and devein the shrimp for you, this recipe is easily ready in the time it takes to cook instant rice—the perfect accompaniment.

2 tablespoons butter or margarine
2 tablespoons minced garlic
1 pound shelled and deveined medium shrimp
  (24 to a pound)
¼ cup dry white wine
¼ cup heavy cream
  Salt and freshly ground pepper

1. Melt the butter in a large frying pan over medium-high heat. Add the garlic and cook, stirring, 1 minute, or until softened and fragrant.

2. Add the shrimp and cook, stirring occasionally, until pink and curled, 3 to 4 minutes. Remove the shrimp to a platter.

3. Add the wine to the skillet and bring to a boil, stirring up any brown bits from the bottom of the pan. Boil over high heat until reduced by half, 1 to 2 minutes. Stir in the cream. Return the shrimp to the pan and boil 1 to 2 minutes longer, until the sauce is slightly thickened and the shrimp are well coated. Season to taste with salt and pepper and serve.

3 TO 4 SERVINGS

QUICK CURRIED SHRIMP

Curry powder adds a sunny color and lively taste to these delicious sautéed shrimp. Serve them over cooked rice.

2 tablespoons butter
1 pound shelled and deveined medium shrimp
  (24 to a pound)
2 tablespoons curry powder
½ cup dry white wine
2 tablespoons garlic herb cheese spread, such as Boursin

1. Melt the butter in a large frying pan over high heat. Add the shrimp and curry powder and cook, stirring frequently, until the shrimp are pink and curled, 2 to 3 minutes.

2. In a small bowl, combine the wine and herb cheese. Mix until smooth and blended. Stir this mixture into the shrimp and warm through. Serve immediately.

3 TO 4 SERVINGS

SHRIMP WITH TEQUILA

Here's a zesty shrimp dish with all the wonderful flavors of the Southwest. Fresh lime wedges would make a nice garnish, both for color and to squeeze over the fish.

2 garlic cloves
2 tablespoons butter
1 pound shelled and deveined large shrimp
  (18 to 20 per pound)
¼ cup tequila
¼ cup chopped cilantro

1. Mince the garlic. Melt the butter in a large frying pan over medium-high heat. Add the garlic and cook, stirring, until the garlic just beings to color, 1 to 2 minutes.

2. Add the shrimp. Cook, stirring, until the shrimp are pink and curled, about 3 minutes.

3. Pour in the tequila and add the cilantro. Heat through and serve.

3 SERVINGS

BROILED FILLET OF SOLE WITH GREEN OLIVE PASTE

Pimiento-stuffed green olives pureed with a little garlic, Parmesan cheese and olive oil make a wonderful sauce for broiled, baked or poached fish. This same blend is also delicious with boiled new potatoes or spread on thin slices of toasted French bread.

1 large garlic clove
1 jar (5 ounces) pimiento-stuffed green olives
¼ cup olive oil
¼ cup grated Parmesan cheese
8 small sole fillets (about 1½ pounds total)

1. Preheat the broiler. Place the garlic clove in a food processor or blender and process until finely chopped. Drain the olives and add them to the processor. Pulse several times to chop them. Then add the olive oil and cheese and process until the olive paste is fairly smooth.

2. Arrange the slices of sole on a broiler pan in a single layer. Spread a thin layer of the olive paste over each fish fillet. Refrigerate any extra olive paste to serve at another time. It keeps well in a covered jar in the refrigerator for up to a week.

3. Broil the fillets 3 to 4 inches from the heat without turning for about 4 minutes, until the fish flakes easily.

4 SERVINGS

POACHED RED SNAPPER WITH TARRAGON BUTTER SAUCE

The great thing about poaching fish is that you can make a sauce quickly by thickening the richly flavored poaching liquid with a little butter.

1½ pounds red snapper fillets
1 shallot
½ cup white wine or clam juice
1 teaspoon dried tarragon leaves
8 tablespoons (1 stick) butter

1. Cut the snapper into 4 equal pieces. Mince the shallot. Place the shallot and wine in a nonreactive, large frying pan. Bring to a boil over high heat.

2. Add the snapper fillets and cook over medium-high heat, turning once, until they are opaque throughout, 5 to 6 minutes total cooking time. Remove the fish to a serving platter.

3. Stir the tarragon into the poaching liquid. Boil over high heat until the liquid is reduced by half, 1 to 2 minutes. Reduce the heat to low and add the butter, 1 tablespoon at a time, whisking constantly. As soon as the butter is incorporated into the sauce, pour the sauce over the fish and serve.

4 SERVINGS

BAKED SNAPPER IN MUSTARD SAUCE

Almost any fish can be substituted for the snapper fillets in this easy recipe.

½ cup sour cream
2 teaspoons Dijon mustard
2 teaspoons lemon juice
4 snapper fillets (5 to 6 ounces each)
⅓ cup minced chives

1. Preheat the oven to 400 degrees F. In a small bowl, combine the sour cream, mustard and lemon juice. Stir to blend well. Lightly coat both sides of each fish fillet with the sour cream mixture. Place the fish in a baking pan just large enough to hold the fillets in a single layer.

2. Sprinkle the chives over the fish. Bake 8 to 10 minutes, until the fish is opaque throughout. If desired, place the fish under the broiler for 1 to 2 minutes to brown lightly before serving.

4 SERVINGS

BAKED SNAPPER WITH TOMATOES AND CAPERS

Baking is a terrific method for cooking fish. In this recipe, a sauce made with fresh ripe tomatoes bastes the snapper as it bakes. Any fish fillet can be substituted for the Pacific snapper.

4 Pacific or red snapper fillets (5 to 6 ounces each)
   Salt and freshly ground pepper
2 medium fresh ripe tomatoes
1½ teaspoons tiny (nonpareil) capers
1½ teaspoons lemon juice
1 teaspoon dried oregano leaves

1. Preheat the oven to 400 degrees F. Place the snapper in a single layer in a small baking dish. Season with salt and pepper to taste.

2. Cut the tomatoes in half and squeeze out the seeds. Then chop coarsely. Combine the tomatoes, capers, lemon juice and oregano and spoon the mixture over the fish.

3. Bake the fish for about 8 minutes, until opaque throughout.

4 SERVINGS

CRISPY POTATO CRUST TROUT

Because trout is farm raised, we can enjoy quick, delicious entrees such as this lemon-chive flavored fish all year round. Of course, it's best right out of the stream.

2 boneless whole trout (about 10 ounces each)
3 tablespoons butter
2 tablespoons fresh lemon juice
2 tablespoons minced fresh chives
1 cup dehydrated instant potato flakes

1. Preheat the broiler. Rinse the trout well. Open up the fish so the fillets lie flat. Cut off the heads and fins.

2. Cut the butter into small pieces. Place in a microwave-safe pie plate and microwave on High until melted, about 1 minute. Stir the lemon juice and chives into the butter.

3. Pour the potato flakes onto a flat plate. Dip both sides of each fish in the lemon butter, then dredge in the potato flakes to coat. Place skin side down on a broiler pan. Spoon any excess potato flakes over the top. Pat down gently.

4. Broil about 4 inches from the heat without turning, for 3 to 5 minutes, until the trout flakes easily and the potatoes are golden brown.

2 SERVINGS

6 PASTA

It usually takes longer to bring the water to a boil than it does to cook the pasta and prepare the sauce. To speed up the process, start a covered pot of water cooking before you even take off your jacket. Also, salt the water *after* it has come to a boil.

There are hundreds of sizes, shapes, flavors and brands of pasta on the market, and the length of cooking time varies slightly with each one. Cooking times even vary between brands for the same size and shape of pasta. It's a good idea to check the labels before you make your purchase.

The recipes in this chapter range from Ravioli with a wonderful Walnut Cream Sauce to Pasta with Sun-Dried Tomatoes and Broccoli. One of our favorite discoveries was to find that it's possible to make Macaroni and Cheese in 10 minutes with only 5 ingredients.

PASTA WITH SUN-DRIED TOMATOES AND BROCCOLI

This one-pot meal has all the colors and flavors of sunny Italy.

1 pound broccoli florets
1 pound fresh fettuccine
1 jar (4 ounces) marinated sun-dried tomatoes
1 tablespoon dried Italian herb seasoning or fines herbes
1 cup freshly grated Parmesan cheese
  Salt and freshly ground pepper

1. In a large pot of boiling salted water, cook the broccoli florets 2 minutes. Add the pasta and continue cooking 2 to 3 minutes longer, until the pasta and broccoli are tender but still firm. Remove from the heat and drain in a colander.

2. While broccoli and pasta are cooking, cut sun-dried tomato pieces in half.

3. Place hot pasta and broccoli in a large serving bowl. Add the tomatoes and some of the oil in which they were marinated, if desired. Toss gently. Sprinkle on the herbs and toss again.

4. Serve immediately. Let each person add grated cheese, salt and pepper, as desired.

4 SERVINGS

LINGUINE WITH CLAM SAUCE

1 pound linguine
3 garlic cloves
3 cans (10 ounces each) baby clams in clam juice
3 tablespoons butter
2 tablespoons flour

1. In a large pot of boiling salted water, cook the linquine until tender but still firm, 8 to 10 minutes.

2. Meanwhile, finely chop the garlic. Drain the clams, reserving the clam juice.

3. Melt the butter in a medium saucepan. Add the garlic and cook over medium heat for 1 minute. Stir in the flour and cook, stirring, for 1 to 2 minutes, without allowing the flour to color. Whisk in the clam juice. Raise the heat to medium-high and bring to a boil, whisking frequently, until the sauce is thickened, 1 to 2 minutes. Reduce the heat to medium-low. Add the clams and simmer for 2 minutes.

4. Drain the cooked pasta and transfer it to a serving bowl. Pour the clam sauce over the pasta and toss until well coated. Serve at once.

4 SERVINGS

PASTA SHELLS WITH CORN AND CHICKEN

Conchigliette, small seashell-shaped pasta, capture the creamy corn and chicken sauce. All you need is a green salad to complete a hearty meal. Use leftover roasted or poached chicken for this recipe or buy some cooked chicken from your supermarket deli or favorite take-out food shop.

1 pound small pasta shells (conchigliette)
1½ cups heavy cream
½ cup grated Parmesan cheese
2 cups diced cooked chicken (about 1 pound)
1¼ cups corn kernels, fresh, frozen or canned
Salt and freshly ground pepper

1. In a large pot of boiling salted water, cook the conchigliette until tender but still firm, 8 to 9 minutes.

2. Meanwhile, heat the cream in a medium saucepan. When the cream is hot but not boiling, stir in the cheese. Add the chicken and corn and heat through. Season with salt and pepper to taste.

3. Drain the pasta and pour into a serving bowl. Pour the sauce over the pasta and toss gently, until the pasta is well coated with the sauce.

4 SERVINGS

FUSILLI WITH SAUTÉED EGGPLANT AND FETA CHEESE

Depending on the brand of pasta you buy, it takes anywhere from 6 to 12 minutes to cook fusilli—so it's important to read the package directions carefully.

1 pound fusilli
½ pound feta cheese
1 medium eggplant
¼ cup extra virgin olive oil
3 cups chunky spaghetti sauce

1. In a large pot of boiling salted water, cook the fusilli until tender but still firm.

2. While the fusilli is cooking, cut the feta cheese into ½-inch dice and set aside. It's not necessary to be exact, and don't worry if the feta crumbles.

3. Cut the eggplant into ¾-inch dice. Heat the oil in a large, heavy frying pan. Add the eggplant cubes and cook, stirring frequently, until the eggplant softens and begin to brown, about 5 minutes. Stir in the spaghetti sauce and feta cheese and heat through.

4. Drain the pasta. Toss gently with the sauce and serve.

4 SERVINGS

FETTUCCINE WITH FRESH ASPARAGUS AND HAM

Substitute broccoli florets when asparagus isn't in season.

  1 pound medium-size fresh asparagus
  1 pound cooked ham
  1 pound fresh fettuccine
1½ cups heavy cream
  1 cup freshly grated Parmesan cheese
    Freshly ground pepper

1. Gently bend each asparagus stalk—it will break at the right point. Save the woody ends for soup and cut the tender asparagus tops (or tips) on a diagonal into lengths about 2 inches long. Cut the ham into thin strips about ¼ inch wide and 1 inch long.

2. Put the asparagus into a large pot of boiling salted water. Cook for 3 minutes. Stir in the fettuccine and cook for 2 to 3 minutes longer, until both asparagus and pasta are tender but still firm. Immediately pour into a colander to drain off the water.

3. Return the pasta and asparagus to the pot. Add the ham, cream, and ½ cup of the Parmesan cheese. Cook, tossing gently, until heated through, about 2 minutes. Serve immediately with the remaining Parmesan cheese and a generous grinding of pepper sprinkled on top.

4 SERVINGS

MEXICALI MACARONI

This hearty one-dish meal is popular with everyone.

1½ cups dried elbow macaroni
1¼ pounds lean ground beef
  1 can (11 ounces) Mexican-style corn
  1 cup chopped ripe tomatoes, fresh or canned
  1 tablespoon chili powder

1. In a large pot of boiling salted water cook the macaroni until tender but still firm, about 5 minutes.

2. While the macaroni is cooking, brown the beef in a frying pan over high heat, stirring occasionally. When the meat is brown, drain off the fat.

3. Add the corn, tomatoes and chili powder to the meat. Heat through, stirring occasionally.

4. When the macaroni is cooked, drain and pour into a serving bowl. Pour the sauce over the macaroni and stir until the ingredients are well combined; then serve.

4 SERVINGS

MACARONI AND CHEESE

1 package (1 pound) elbow macaroni
4 cups milk (use skim or 1 percent if you like)
8 tablespoons (1 stick) butter
½ cup flour
1 pound shredded sharp Cheddar cheese (4 cups)

1. In a large pot of boiling salted water, cook the macaroni until tender but still firm, 4 to 5 minutes.

2. While the pasta is cooking, preheat the broiler. Pour the milk into a 1-quart glass or ceramic bowl and heat in the microwave on High for 3 minutes.

3. Melt the butter in a large, heavy saucepan over medium-high heat. Whisk in the flour and cook, stirring, for 1 to 2 minutes to make a roux. Whisk in the hot milk and bring to a boil, whisking until thickened and smooth, 2 to 3 minutes. Stir in 3 cups of the cheese. Season the sauce with salt and pepper to taste.

4. Drain the pasta and add it to the sauce, stirring gently to mix. Turn the macaroni and cheese into a buttered 9- by 13-inch flameproof baking dish or gratin. Sprinkle the remaining cheese over the top. Broil for about 2 minutes, until the cheese melts.

6 TO 8 SERVINGS

PASTA WITH PEPPERS AND PESTO

For the most colorful effect, use a variety of red, yellow and green peppers. A pesto made with a generous dose of garlic works especially well in this dish.

1 pound rotelle
3 sweet bell peppers (preferably red, yellow and green)
1 large red onion
3 tablespoons olive oil
1 cup pesto

1. In a large pot of boiling salted water, cook the rotelle until tender but still firm, 8 to 9 minutes.

2. While the pasta is cooking, thinly slice the peppers and the red onion. Heat the olive oil in a large frying pan. Add the peppers and onion and cook over high heat, stirring occasionally, until the peppers begin to soften, about 3 minutes. Reduce the heat to low, cover and let the vegetables simmer until the pasta is done.

3. Scoop out and reserve ½ cup of the pasta cooking water. Drain the pasta into a colander and transfer to a large serving bowl. Add the pesto and the reserved cooking water and toss until the pasta is well coated with the sauce. Pour the peppers and onion over the pasta, toss again and serve.

4 TO 6 SERVINGS

FASTA PASTA PUTTANESCA

The important ingredient in this earthy pasta sauce is olives. Oil-cured black olives are best for this recipe, although they do have to be pitted. A good alternative is to buy imported pitted kalamata olives. A prepared marinara sauce is fine to use in this recipe as long as it's well seasoned with garlic.

1 pound spaghetti
3 cups chunky marinara sauce with garlic
¾ cup pitted oil-cured or kalamata olives
¼ cup tiny (nonpareil) capers
8 flat anchovy fillets

1. In a large pot of boiling salted water, cook the spaghetti according to package directions until tender but still firm, about 8 to 10 minutes.

2. Meanwhile, in a saucepan, combine the marinara sauce with the olives and capers. Cook over medium heat, stirring, until heated through.

3. When the pasta is done, drain and transfer to a large serving platter. Spoon the warm sauce over the pasta and garnish with the anchovy fillets.

4 SERVINGS

RAVIOLI IN WALNUT CREAM SAUCE

This dish is wonderful, although very rich. We're more likely to serve it for a first course than for an entree. It doesn't matter whether you use chicken, veal or beef ravioli or if it's fresh, refrigerated or frozen as long as it's high quality.

1 package (1 pound) meat-stuffed ravioli
1 cup walnut pieces
1¼ cups heavy cream
½ cup grated Parmesan cheese
2 tablespoons finely chopped parsley

1. In a large pot of boiling salted water, cook the ravioli according to package directions just until tender but still firm, about 7 minutes.

2. Place the walnuts in a food processor and process until they are finely ground.

3. Heat the cream in a saucepan. Stir in the ground walnuts and Parmesan cheese. Heat through, being careful that the cream doesn't boil.

4. When the ravioli are done, drain off the water and pour them into a serving bowl. Pour the sauce over the ravioli and sprinkle on the parsley. Serve immediately.

4 MAIN-COURSE OR 6 FIRST-COURSE SERVINGS

ROTELLE WITH FETA, CHOPPED TOMATOES AND OLIVES

If you can find fresh mozzarella cheese, use it instead of the feta in this recipe for wagon wheel–shaped pasta.

1 pound rotelle
1 cup pitted ripe olives
½ pound feta cheese
¼ cup extra virgin olive oil
1 can (28 ounces) crushed tomatoes with added puree

1. In a large pot of boiling salted water, cook the rotelle until tender but still firm, about 7 minutes.

2. While the pasta is cooking, coarsely chop the olives. Crumble the feta cheese.

3. Heat the oil in a large, heavy frying pan. When the oil is hot, stir in the tomatoes with their juices, the olives and the cheese. Gently warm through. Reduce the heat to low and keep warm.

4. Drain the cooked pasta and pour it into a serving bowl. Pour the sauce over the pasta and toss gently to coat well.

4 SERVINGS

ALL SAINTS' PASTA

Too bad sardines are so often overlooked. We always keep a few tins in our pantry, because they're great in so many recipes.

½ pound fettuccine, fresh or dried
1 pound medium zucchini (about 3)
1 large garlic clove
4 tins (3¾ ounces each) sardines packed in olive oil
2 large ripe tomatoes, chopped, or 1 can (14 ounces) Italian peeled tomatoes, drained and chopped

1. In a large pot of boiling salted water, cook the fettuccine until tender but still firm, 2 to 3 minutes for fresh, 5 to 7 for dried.

2. Meanwhile, trim the zucchini. Quarter each lengthwise, then slice thinly crosswise. Mince the garlic.

3. Drain the sardines, reserving the oil. Heat 3 tablespoons of the reserved oil in a large frying pan. Add the zucchini and garlic and cook over medium-high heat, stirring frequently, until the zucchini is tender, about 4 minutes. Add the tomatoes and sardines and heat through.

4. Drain the pasta and transfer to a serving bowl. Pour the sauce over the pasta and toss gently to combine ingredients. Serve immediately.

2 TO 3 SERVINGS

ANGEL HAIR PASTA TOPPED
WITH TAPENADE

This zesty puree of ripe olives, fruity olive oil, garlic and
Parmesan cheese is delicious over angel hair pasta. If you have
any left over, spread it on broiled fish or crusty bread. Be sure to
cover the saucepan of water so it will come to a boil faster.

```
1 can (6 ounces) ripe black olives
1 large garlic clove
½ cup grated Parmesan cheese
¼ cup extra virgin olive oil
   Salt
12 ounces angel hair pasta
```

1. Bring a large pot of water to a boil over high heat. Meanwhile,
drain the olives. Chop the garlic in a food processor or blender.
Add the olives, cheese and olive oil to the food processor and
puree until the mixture is smooth.

2. When the water in the pot begins to boil, salt generously. Add
the angel hair pasta and cook uncovered until tender but still
firm, 2 to 3 minutes. Drain the pasta in a colander; then transfer
to a serving bowl. Add the olive puree and toss until well coated.

4 SERVINGS

VODKA AND RED PEPPER SAUCE PASTA WITH FRESH BASIL

This mild-looking sauce is a tad deceiving. Red pepper flakes soaked in vodka add a generous measure of heat.

⅓ cup vodka
1 to 2 teaspoons hot red pepper flakes, to taste
1 pound fresh or dried plain or spinach fettuccine
1 can (28 ounces) crushed tomatoes with added puree
1 cup loosely packed basil leaves
½ teaspoon salt

1. Combine the vodka and red pepper flakes; let stand for 5 minutes. Then strain, discarding the red pepper flakes.

2. In a large pot of boiling salted water, cook the fettuccine just until tender but still firm, 2 to 3 minutes for fresh, 5 to 7 minutes for dried.

3. Place the tomatoes and their juices, along with the basil, in a 2-quart glass or ceramic bowl. Stir in the flavored vodka. Place in the microwave oven and cook on High for 2 to 3 minutes, until heated through.

4. Drain the pasta, transfer to a serving bowl and pour the tomato-basil sauce over it; toss until mixed.

4 SERVINGS

FETTUCCINE WITH SWISS CHARD

Any flavor of fettuccine can be used in this recipe. If you like, serve with grated Parmesan cheese.

2 packages (10 ounces each) frozen chopped Swiss chard
2 large garlic cloves
¼ cup extra virgin olive oil
1 can (14½ ounces) chicken broth
1 pound fresh fettuccine

1. Place the Swiss chard in a colander. Run cold water over the chard to thaw; then squeeze out the excess liquid. Mince the garlic cloves.

2. Heat the olive oil in a large frying pan. Add the garlic and chard and cook, stirring, for 1 to 2 minutes. Add the chicken broth and heat through.

3. In a large pot of boiling salted water, cook the fettuccine just until tender but still firm, about 2 to 3 minutes. Drain in a colander and pour into a serving bowl. Pour the Swiss chard sauce over the fettuccine and toss until well mixed.

4 TO 6 SERVINGS

NOODLES ITALIANO

Dress quick-cooking egg noodles with your best extra virgin olive oil and mixed Italian herbs for one of the fastest side-dish pastas imaginable.

½ pound egg noodles
¼ cup extra virgin olive oil
2 tablespoons dried Italian herb seasoning or fines herbes
1 cup freshly grated Parmesan cheese
Freshly ground black pepper

1. In a large pot of boiling salted water, cook the egg noodles until tender but still firm. Depending on the brand of noodles you buy, the total cooking time will range from 3 to 6 minutes.

2. Pour into a colander to drain off the water. Place the noodles in a serving bowl and gently toss with the olive oil and herbs.

3. Serve immediately. Let everyone add cheese and freshly ground pepper to his or her own taste.

4 SERVINGS

QUICK NOODLE PUDDING

This streamlined sweet "kugel" casserole makes a great nutritious dessert or a brunch dish.

1 package (12 ounces) wide egg noodles
1 carton (1 pint) small-curd cottage cheese
1 cup sour cream
½ cup plus 2 tablespoons firmly packed brown sugar
2 tablespoons butter

1. Preheat the broiler. Butter an 8-inch square baking pan. Cook the egg noodles in a large pot of boiling salted water, according to package directions, just until tender but still firm, about 5 minutes. Drain the noodles in a colander, then return them to the pot.

2. Stir in the cottage cheese, sour cream and ½ cup of the sugar. Pour the noodle mixture into the buttered pan. Sprinkle the remaining sugar and the butter, cut into small pieces, on top of the noodles. Place the casserole under the broiler about 3 inches from the heat and broil for 3 to 4 minutes, until the top is crispy and golden brown.

4 TO 6 SERVINGS

7 VEGETABLES AND SIDE DISHES

As eating habits change for the better, vegetables are gaining more importance. Rather than merely garnishing a meat entree, vegetables in many cases are becoming the main event.

When purchasing vegetables the important thing to remember is that they are always best when grown locally and bought fresh in season. Vegetables picked ripe will have more flavor and be more tender than those picked a week before and shipped long distances. Young fresh green beans, for example, cook in less than 10 minutes compared to out-of-season beans, which tend to be tough and consequently take longer to prepare.

Zucchini and other summer squashes, tomatoes, eggplant, corn, asparagus, bell peppers, mushrooms and cabbage all lend themselves to 10-minute recipes. There are unlimited possibilities, including Asparagus with Warm Tomato Vinaigrette, Garlicky Eggplant and Zucchini, and Red Cabbage and Apples in Caraway Cream Sauce.

ASPARAGUS WITH
WARM TOMATO VINAIGRETTE

If you're a purist, you may want to peel the tomatoes, which
is easy to do. Just plunge them into boiling water for 10 to
20 seconds and then slip off the skins.

> 1 pound fresh asparagus
> 2 medium-size ripe tomatoes
>   Salt
> 3 tablespoons extra virgin olive oil
> 1½ tablespoons tarragon white wine vinegar
> ½ teaspoon honey

1. Bend the bottom part of each asparagus spear until it breaks
naturally. Rinse the tender spears. Discard the tough part.

2. Pour about 1 inch of water into a large frying pan and bring to
a boil over high heat. Meanwhile, cut the tomatoes in half and
squeeze out the seeds. Coarsely chop the tomatoes.

3. Generously salt the boiling water. Add the asparagus, return
the water to a boil and cook until tender, 3 to 5 minutes.

4. Heat the olive oil in a nonreactive, small saucepan. Stir in the
vinegar and honey. Add the tomatoes and heat through. Drain the
asparagus and arrange on a platter. Pour the sauce over the
asparagus. Serve warm or at room temperature.

4 SERVINGS

BAKED STUFFED AVOCADOS

Baked avocado stuffed with creamy rice studded with currants and pine nuts makes a wonderful vegetarian first course or lunch dish.

¾ cup quick-cooking rice
¼ teaspoon salt
2 ripe avocados
¼ cup pine nuts (pignoli)
2 tablespoons currants or raisins
2 tablespoons sour cream

1. Preheat the oven to 400 degrees F. Pour ¾ cup water into a small saucepan and bring to a boil. Stir in the rice and salt; cover and let stand for 5 minutes.

2. While the rice is cooking, cut the avocados in half and remove the pits. Scoop out most of the flesh, leaving a thin shell of avocado in the peel. Mash the avocado. Stir in the pine nuts, currants and sour cream. Then stir in the hot rice.

3. Mound the rice filling in each of the avocado halves. Bake for 5 minutes. Serve the stuffed avocados warm or at room temperature.

4 SERVINGS

CARROT PILAF

Chopped dried apricots give an interesting chewy texture and a touch of sweetness to this quick carrot sauté. Shredding the carrots in the food processor saves a lot of time.

1 pound carrots (about 4 medium)
3 tablespoons butter
⅓ cup lime or lemon juice
4 ounces dried apricot halves (about 1 cup)
¼ cup firmly packed brown sugar

1. Coarsely shred the carrots on the shredding disc of a food processor. Melt the butter in a nonreactive, large frying pan. Stir in the carrots and lime juice. Cover and let cook for 3 to 4 minutes over medium-high heat, until the carrots begin to soften.

2. Meanwhile, coarsely chop the apricots. Stir the chopped apricots and brown sugar into the carrots and cook, stirring occasionally, for 4 to 5 minutes longer, until the carrots just begin to brown. Serve warm.

4 SERVINGS

CORN CAKES

Serve these savory corn cakes with baked ham or barbecued chicken. Both are available already prepared. We also like to serve these crispy corn cakes with eggs for brunch.

1 can (16½ ounces) cream-style corn
½ cup flour
⅓ cup minced chives
1 egg
3 tablespoons oil

1. In a medium bowl, combine the cream-style corn, flour, chives and egg. Beat until well blended.

2. Heat a large, heavy frying pan, preferably cast-iron, over medium-high heat. Add about 2 tablespoons of the oil. When the oil is hot, gently drop in the batter by heaping tablespoons and cook the cakes until the bottoms are golden brown, about 1 minute. Turn the corn cakes over and brown on the other side. Repeat, using up all of the batter, and adding the remaining oil if the skillet becomes dry. Serve hot.

4 SERVINGS

GARLICKY EGGPLANT AND ZUCCHINI

This quick sauté is a great vegetable dish to serve with broiled fish or roast chicken. And it's just as good served cold as it is served hot. Although we normally reserve our fruitiest olive oil for salads or to drizzle over bread, a rich olive flavor is important to the success of this dish.

1 small eggplant (about ¾ pound)
4 small zucchini (about ¾ pound)
2 garlic cloves
3 tablespoons extra virgin olive oil
½ teaspoon salt
¼ teaspoon freshly ground pepper

1. Cut the eggplant into ½-inch cubes. Cut the zucchini into ½-inch slices. Chop the garlic.

2. Heat the olive oil in a large frying pan. Add the garlic and cook over medium heat until softened and fragrant, about 1 minute. Add the eggplant and zucchini, raise the heat to high and cook, stirring occasionally, until the vegetables begin to brown, about 8 minutes longer. Season with the salt and pepper. Serve hot or at room temperature.

4 SERVINGS

JAPANESE EGGPLANT WITH ONIONS AND MINT

Fresh mint adds interesting flavor to Japanese eggplant.

2 Japanese eggplant (about 6 inches long)
3 tablespoons olive oil
1 small onion
3 tablespoons chopped fresh mint
3 tablespoons sour cream

1. Preheat the broiler. Cut the eggplant in half lengthwise. Drizzle ¾ teaspoon of olive oil over the cut surface of each half. Place skin-side down on a broiler pan and broil about 4 inches from the heat until tender, 3 to 4 minutes.

2. Chop the onion. Heat the remaining 2 tablespoons of oil in a medium frying pan. Add the onion and cook over high heat, stirring, until the onion begins to brown, about 4 minutes.

3. Add the mint and sour cream to the onion and stir to mix. Spoon the onion mixture over the eggplant halves and return them to the broiler for 1 minute, or until hot and bubbly on top.

4 SERVINGS

BRAZILIAN GREENS WITH ORANGE

This dish goes well with smoked and roasted meat and chicken.

1 bunch of Swiss chard (about 1½ pounds)
3 tablespoons butter
⅔ cup orange juice
1 orange

1. Separate the leaves from the stems of the Swiss chard. (Reserve the stems to use in another recipe, see page 152.) Roll up all of the leaves in a bundle, then cut crosswise with a large, sharp knife into 1- to 1½-inch pieces. Rinse the chard.

2. Melt 2 tablespoons of the butter in a large frying pan over medium-high heat. Add the chard and cook, stirring frequently, for about 3 minutes, until the chard is wilted. Stir in the orange juice, reduce the heat to medium and cook, stirring occasionally, until the chard is tender, about 4 minutes longer.

3. Meanwhile, peel the orange and cut it into thin slices.

4. When the chard is done, remove it from the pan with a slotted spoon. Increase the heat to high and boil rapidly to reduce the sauce slightly, about 2 minutes. Arrange the orange slices over the chard. Swirl 1 tablespoon butter into the orange sauce, pour it over the chard and serve.

4 SERVINGS

GREEN BEANS WITH PEANUT SAUCE

This creamy Indonesian-inspired peanut sauce turns plain green beans into something special.

1 bag (1 pound) frozen French-cut green beans
2 large garlic cloves
1 can (13½ ounces) unsweetened coconut milk
¼ cup chunky peanut butter
1 tablespoon soy sauce

1. Place the green beans plus 3 tablespoons water in a microwave-safe casserole. Cover and microwave on High for 7½ minutes, stirring the beans halfway through the cooking time.

2. Meanwhile, prepare the peanut sauce. Mince the garlic or crush it through a press and set aside. Pour the coconut milk into a medium saucepan. Whisk in the peanut butter until smooth. Then stir in the soy sauce and garlic.

3. Drain the beans and spoon into a serving dish. Pour the peanut sauce over the beans and serve.

6 SERVINGS

BABY LIMAS WITH SAUSAGE AND TOMATOES

Frozen baby lima beans are a great convenience food. Cook them and puree with a little cream, butter and lemon zest for an interesting side dish, add to vegetable sautés or combine with chopped tomatoes and sausage. Serve over noodles or rice.

1 package (10 ounces) frozen baby lima beans
1 large ripe fresh tomato
1 bunch of green onions (about 6)
6 ounces fresh pork sausage with sage (half of a
    12-ounce tube)

1. Place the lima beans in a 1-quart glass or ceramic casserole. Add ¼ cup water. Cover and microwave on High for 5 minutes.

2. Meanwhile, cut the tomato in half. Squeeze out the seeds, then chop coarsely. Trim the root end and most of the tops from the green onions. Rinse the onions, then mince.

3. Cook the sausage in a large frying pan over high heat, stirring occasionally, until it begins to brown. Add the green onions and tomatoes and cook, stirring, until the vegetables are softened, 2 to 3 minutes. Stir in the drained lima beans and serve.

4 SERVINGS

MARVELOUS MUSHROOMS

The trick to these flavorful mushrooms is to cook them quickly, before they begin to lose any moisture. They are delicious spooned over thin slices of lightly toasted French or Italian bread, broiled chicken breasts, grilled steaks, even cooked rice or pasta.

    1 pound mushrooms
  10 garlic cloves
    2 tablespoons vegetable oil
    2 tablespoons soy sauce
    1 tablespoon finely chopped fresh parsley

1. Wipe the mushrooms. Cut a thin slice off the stem ends. If the mushrooms are large, cut them in quarters. Finely chop the garlic (or to save time, use about 2½ tablespoons prepared chopped garlic).

2. Heat the oil in a large frying pan. Add the chopped garlic and cook over medium-low heat, stirring occasionally, until golden, 4 to 6 minutes. Be careful not to let the garlic burn.

3. Increase the heat to high. Add the mushrooms and cook, stirring, for 2 to 3 minutes, or just until the mushrooms begin to color. Sprinkle on the soy sauce and serve immediately, garnished with parsley.

4 SERVINGS

MUSHROOMS WITH TRICOLOR PEPPERS

A large gift of wild mushrooms inspired this dish, but the concept works equally well with cultivated white mushrooms. The trick is to cook the mushrooms and sweet bell peppers over very high heat until they just begin to give up their moisture. Serve this as a vegetable side dish or over rice or pasta.

1 pound fresh mushrooms
3 sweet bell peppers (red, green and yellow)
3 tablespoons extra virgin olive oil
3 tablespoons lemon juice
   Salt and freshly ground pepper

1. Wipe the mushrooms and trim a thin slice from the stem ends. Cut them in half if they're large; otherwise leave them whole. Cut the bell peppers in half and remove the stem and any seeds. Cut the peppers into 1½-inch squares.

2. Heat the olive oil in a large frying pan. Add the mushrooms and bell peppers and cook over high heat, stirring occasionally, until the mushrooms just begin to give up some moisture, about 5 minutes.

3. Sprinkle the lemon juice over the vegetables and season to taste with salt and pepper. Serve hot.

6 SERVINGS

OKRA AND CORN STEW WITH SHRIMP

Cooked this way, okra stays crisp. Serve this colorful dish with sautéed catfish or fried chicken. It's a Southern treat.

1 package (1 pound 4 ounces) frozen okra
2 whole pimientos
2 tablespoons butter
1 can (16 ounces) whole-kernel corn, drained
½ pound cooked baby shrimp
    Salt and freshly ground pepper

1. Place the okra in a glass bowl, cover with microwave-safe plastic wrap and microwave on High for 3 minutes. Meanwhile, cut the pimientos into small dice.

2. Melt the butter in a large frying pan over medium-high heat. Add the corn, pimientos and okra and cook, stirring occasionally, for 3 minutes. Stir in the shrimp and cook 2 minutes longer. Season with salt and pepper to taste. Serve hot.

6 TO 8 SERVINGS

POTATO TORTILLA

In Spain, a tortilla is a thick egg pancake or omelet. Using canned sliced potatoes is the secret to preparing this savory brunch dish in 10 minutes. You can vary the recipe by substituting shredded zucchini or sliced roasted sweet red peppers for the potatoes. If you use a frying pan with a flameproof handle, you can slide the tortilla under the broiler for a minute or two to finish the cooking, rather than inverting it.

1 can (16 ounces) sliced potatoes
1 small onion
3 tablespoons olive oil
12 eggs
Salt and pepper

1. Drain the potatoes. Thinly slice the onion.

2. Heat the olive oil in a 10-inch nonstick or well-seasoned cast-iron frying pan. Add the onion and cook over medium heat, stirring occasionally, until the slices are translucent, about 2 minutes.

3. Add the potato slices and cook until heated through, 1 to 2 minutes. Beat the eggs until frothy. Season with salt and pepper to taste.

4. Pour the beaten eggs over the potatoes and onion. Cook over medium-high heat, lifting the edges of the tortilla with a spatula to allow the uncooked egg to flow under, until the bottom two-thirds is set, about 3 minutes. Place a large plate over the skillet and invert. Quickly slide the tortilla back into the skillet and continue cooking until cooked through, 1 to 2 minutes longer.

6 SERVINGS

QUICK RATATOUILLE

Who says ratatouille, the popular vegetable dish from Provence, has to slowly simmer for an hour or more? This 10-minute version is delicious served hot, cold or at room temperature. We like it as a vegetable side dish with roast chicken or as an appetizer spooned on slices of bread or crackers. It also makes a great omelet filling.

1 small eggplant (about 1 pound)
1 medium onion
2 cans (16 ounces each) zucchini in tomato sauce
2 tablespoons tiny (nonpareil) capers
¼ cup vinaigrette or bottled Italian salad dressing

1. Trim off the stem end of the eggplant. Cut the eggplant into 1-inch cubes. Coarsely chop the onion. In a nonreactive, medium saucepan, combine the eggplant, onion, and zucchini with its sauce. Bring the mixture to a simmer over high heat. Cook, stirring occasionally, until the eggplant is tender, about 6 minutes.

2. Stir in the capers and continue cooking for 2 minutes longer. Remove from the heat and stir in the vinaigrette.

8 SERVINGS

RED CABBAGE AND APPLES IN CARAWAY CREAM SAUCE

If ever a recipe can taste like a season, it's this one, which reminds everyone in my family of autumn.

½ of a small red cabbage (about 1 pound)
2 tart apples
2 tablespoons vegetable oil
1 cup heavy cream
1 teaspoon caraway seeds
Salt and freshly ground pepper

1. Place the cabbage, cut side down, on a cutting board. With a large stainless steel knife, slice it into very thin shreds. Quarter the apples. Remove the cores and cut the apples into ½-inch dice.

2. Heat the oil in a large frying pan. Add the cabbage and apples and cook over high heat, stirring frequently, until the cabbage wilts, about 6 minutes.

3. Stir in the cream and caraway seeds. Cook for 3 to 4 minutes longer, until the cream begins to thicken. Season with salt and pepper to taste. Serve hot.

6 TO 8 SERVINGS

SAUSAGE-STUFFED ZUCCHINI

Serve this pretty dish as a vegetable accompaniment or cut into pieces and serve as an appetizer.

2 medium zucchini
3 green onions
6 ounces fresh pork sausage with sage (half of a
   12-ounce tube)
1 pimiento
2 tablespoons dry bread crumbs

1. Preheat the broiler. Trim the stem end off each of the zucchini, then slice in half lengthwise. With a paring knife, make a shallow V-cut in the zucchini to remove some of the inside, leaving a ¼-inch-thick shell.

2. Slice the wedges of zucchini that you've removed. Mince the green onions. Mix the onions and sausage together until blended. Fill the zucchini with the sausage. Arrange the zucchini wedges on top. Cut the pimiento in strips and arrange on top of the zucchini as a garnish. Sprinkle on the bread crumbs.

3. Broil about 4 inches from the heat until the sausage and zucchini are cooked through, about 6 minutes.

4 SERVINGS

STUFFED CROOKNECK SQUASH

4 small crookneck squash (3 to 4 ounces each)
1 small onion
½ cup cashews
2 tablespoons butter
½ cup dry herbed bread crumbs

1. Cut the crookneck squash in half lengthwise. Place them in a shallow ceramic or tempered glass baking dish, cover tightly with microwave-safe plastic wrap and cook on High for 3 to 4 minutes, until fork tender.

2. While the squash is cooking, coarsely chop the onion and the cashews. Melt the butter in a medium frying pan. Add the onion and cook over medium heat, stirring occasionally, until the onion is translucent, 2 to 3 minutes. Preheat the broiler.

3. Remove the squash from the microwave. With a spoon, scoop out some of the centers, being careful to leave a ⅜-inch-thick shell. Chop the removed squash and stir into the onion along with the cashews and ¼ cup of the bread crumbs.

4. Fill the squash shells with the stuffing mixture. Sprinkle the remaining bread crumbs on top. Place the stuffed squash on a broiler pan and broil about 4 inches from the heat, until golden brown on top, 2 to 3 minutes.

4 SERVINGS

CRISPY SWISS CHARD STEMS

Most people use Swiss chard leaves but discard the stems, which is really a waste. They're a treat when coated with bread crumbs and cheese and fried.

1 bunch of Swiss chard
3 eggs
1 cup dry bread crumbs
1 cup grated Parmesan cheese (about 4 ounces)
    Approximately ¼ cup vegetable oil

1. Trim the leaves from the chard stems. (Reserve the leaves to use in another recipe; see page 140.) Rinse the stems.

2. Beat the eggs in a shallow bowl until blended. Combine the bread crumbs and cheese in a pie plate and toss to mix. Heat the oil in a large frying pan.

3. Dip the chard stems in the eggs, then dredge in the Parmesan crumbs to coat.

4. As soon as the oil is hot, begin frying the chard stems, about 6 to 8 at a time, being careful not to crowd the pan. When they're brown on one side, about 2 minutes, turn them over and brown the other side. Remove to paper towels to drain. Serve warm.

4 TO 6 SERVINGS

BAKED TOMATOES FILLED WITH SQUASH AND ALMONDS

1 package (10 ounces) frozen cooked squash
6 medium tomatoes (about 1½ pounds)
2 tablespoons firmly packed brown sugar
2 tablespoons butter
3 tablespoons sliced almonds

1. Preheat the oven to 375 degrees F. Place the squash in a 1-quart microwave-safe casserole. Cover and microwave on High for 6 minutes.

2. While the squash is cooking, prepare the tomatoes. Cut a thin slice off the bottom so the tomatoes will stand up. Holding a paring knife at a 45-degree angle, cut around the top of the tomato to hollow out about half of it.

3. Arrange the tomatoes in a small baking dish and place them in the oven. Bake for 4 to 5 minutes, until heated through.

4. When the squash is done, stir in the brown sugar and butter and spoon the mixture into the tomatoes. Sprinkle the almonds on top. Transfer to the broiler and broil about 4 inches from the heat for 1 to 2 minutes, until the nuts are lightly toasted. Serve hot.

6 SERVINGS

CALLOPED TOMATOES

N I

omatoes

ini

... leaves

...ary bread crumbs

2½ tablespoons extra virgin olive oil

Salt and freshly ground pepper

1. Preheat the oven to 500 degrees F. Cut the tomatoes crosswise into ¼-inch slices. Coarsely shred the zucchini using a food processor or a hand grater. In a food processor, combine the basil leaves and bread crumbs. Process until the basil is chopped.

2. Grease a 2-quart gratin dish or shallow casserole with ½ tablespoon of the olive oil. Sprinkle ⅓ of the basil bread crumbs over the bottom of the dish. Arrange half the tomatoes in the dish, overlapping the slices slightly if necessary. Season with salt and pepper to taste. Cover the tomatoes with the shredded zucchini. Sprinkle ½ of the remaining bread crumbs over the zucchini. Arrange the remaining tomato slices on top. Season them with salt and pepper. Top with the remaining bread crumbs. Drizzle the remaining olive oil over the bread crumbs.

3. Bake for 8 to 10 minutes, until the top is nicely browned and the zucchini is tender.

6 SERVINGS

ZUCCHINI PANCAKES

Crisp zucchini pancakes go wonderfully with so many entrees and also make a nice appetizer topped with a dab of sour cream and chives.

1 pound zucchini
3 green onions
1 egg
½ cup flour
½ teaspoon salt
¼ teaspoon pepper
3 tablespoons vegetable oil

1. Coarsely shred the zucchini on the shredding disc of a food processor or on the large holes of a hand grater. Place the zucchini in a medium bowl. Trim off the root ends and most of the tops from the green onions. Mince the rest and add to the zucchini along with the egg, flour, salt and pepper. Stir until well combined.

2. Heat 2 tablespoons of the oil in a large frying pan. When the oil is hot, drop about ¼ cup of batter at a time into the pan to form 3 pancakes about 3½ inches in diameter. Cook until brown on both sides, about 5 minutes total cooking time. Repeat with the remaining oil and batter. Serve 2 per person.

3 SERVINGS

COCONUT RAISIN RICE

This sweet rice dish is the traditional accompaniment to spicy Caribbean curry, but it also makes a nice dessert. If you want to gild the lily, soak the raisins in ¼ cup warm rum before folding them into the hot rice.

    4 tablespoons butter
    ½ teaspoon salt
2¼ cups enriched precooked rice
    ½ cup raisins
    ½ cup shredded coconut
    ⅓ cup firmly packed dark brown sugar

1. Place 2¼ cups water, 1 tablespoon of the butter and the salt in a saucepan and bring to a boil. Stir in the rice. Cover and let stand for 5 minutes.

2. Fluff rice with a fork. Then gently stir in the remaining butter. When the butter is melted, gently stir in the raisins, coconut and brown sugar. Serve warm.

6 SERVINGS

8 DESSERTS

Although 10 minutes doesn't allow enough time to bake cakes and cookies from scratch, there are still dozens of fabulous sweet treats you can pull together in short order.

Most of the *5 in 10* desserts utilize sweet, juicy fresh ripe fruit. This collection of recipes includes a warm Berry Gratin, decadent Caramelized Apples, Glazed Bananas over Coffee Ice Cream, and Peaches with Marzipan and Vanilla Rum Cream. It's even possible to make Fruit Crisp within the time allowed by first heating the fruit in the microwave, then sprinkling on a crushed cookie and nut topping and placing under the broiler for a few minutes to crisp.

Ready-prepared pie crusts, available in both large and individual sizes, are also a terrific timesaver. Fill a chocolate crust with coffee and vanilla ice cream and top with fudge sauce. Another idea is Lemon Cloud Pie. Fold buttery lemon curd into lightly whipped cream. Mound the fluffy mixture into a baked pie shell and top with sliced strawberries. Prepared pound cake (I prefer the kind made with all butter) is also a great convenience for making quick trifles.

CARAMELIZED APPLES

If you served these caramelized apples on a pastry crust it would be like having a right-side-up tarte Tatin. Just as good, and much easier than baking pastry crusts, is to serve the warm apples over vanilla ice cream. The only time-consuming part of this recipe is peeling and coring the apples.

4 tart apples
3 tablespoons butter
⅔ cup sugar
¾ teaspoon apple pie spice or cinnamon
½ cup heavy cream

1. Peel and quarter the apples. Cut out the cores and cut each quarter in half again to make 8 wedges from each apple.

2. Melt the butter in a large frying pan. Add the apples and cook over high heat, stirring with a wooden spoon until the apples begin to soften, about 3 minutes.

3. Sprinkle on the sugar and apple pie spice and continue cooking, still stirring, until the sugar begins to caramelize, about 4 minutes.

4. Stir in the cream and cook until the sauce thickens, 2 to 3 minutes. Serve plain or over ice cream.

4 SERVINGS

GLAZED BANANAS OVER COFFEE ICE CREAM

For a festive touch, add a little rum to the orange glaze.

4 tablespoons butter
1 tablespoon brown sugar
¼ cup orange juice
2 bananas
1 pint coffee ice cream

1. Melt the butter in a medium frying pan. Add the brown sugar and cook, stirring, until the sugar and butter form a syrup. Stir in the orange juice, mixing until well blended.

2. Peel the bananas. Cut in half lengthwise, then cut crosswise in quarters. Add the bananas to the orange syrup and cook, turning gently once or twice, until the bananas are heated through, 1 to 2 minutes.

3. Place a scoop of ice cream in 4 dessert dishes. Spoon the bananas and sauce over the ice cream and serve immediately.

4 SERVINGS

BANANA FRITTERS

Fried bananas are popular in every culture. Serve them with a dusting of powdered sugar, or go for broke and add a scoop of vanilla ice cream.

1 cup flour
½ cup beer
¼ cup vegetable oil
2 ripe bananas
3 tablespoons powdered sugar

1. In a medium bowl, beat the flour and beer together until smooth. Heat the oil in a large frying pan.

2. Peel the bananas. Cut in half lengthwise, then cut each half crosswise in half. Dip the bananas in the batter, being sure to coat all sides.

3. When the oil is hot, add half the bananas and cook over medium-high heat, turning once, until coating is golden brown and crisp, about 3 minutes. Remove to paper towels to drain. Repeat with the remaining bananas.

4. Serve the bananas warm, with a dusting of powdered sugar.

4 SERVINGS

BERRY GRATIN

This is an elegant way to present fresh berries.

3 cups fresh berries
1 cup heavy cream
2 tablespoons sliced almonds
2 tablespoons powdered sugar

1. Preheat the broiler. Rinse and drain the berries and divide them among 4 individual gratin dishes or ramekins.

2. Lightly whip the cream. Spoon the cream over the berries. Sprinkle the almonds over the cream. Then dust with the powdered sugar.

3. Place the gratin dishes under the broiler 3 to 4 inches from the heat and broil for about 2 minutes, until golden brown. Serve warm.

4 SERVINGS

FRESH BERRIES WITH CREAMY ORANGE SAUCE

This light, fluffy dessert sauce is wonderful with any fresh fruit, especially strawberries and blueberries. Grand Mariner is a particularly distinctive orange liqueur. Curaçao, Triple Sec and Cointreau are other choices.

1 package (3 ounces) cream cheese, softened
⅓ cup undiluted frozen orange juice concentrate
⅓ cup milk
2 tablespoons orange-flavored liqueur
1 pint fresh blueberries

1. Place the cream cheese, orange juice concentrate, milk and liqueur in a blender or food processor. Process until smooth.

2. Rinse and drain the blueberries. Divide them among 4 dessert dishes. Spoon the sauce on top of the fruit and serve.

4 SERVINGS

SAUTÉED RASPBERRIES IN PORT

When berries are plentiful, this is one of our favorite ways to enjoy them.

3 cups raspberries (preferably fresh, although frozen
   berries can be substituted)
2 tablespoons butter
1 tablespoon sugar
¼ cup port
1 pint vanilla ice cream

1. Rinse the berries and drain well. Melt the butter in a medium frying pan over medium-high heat.

2. Add the berries and stir gently to coat with the butter. Sprinkle the sugar over the berries. Then pour in the port and warm through.

3. Place a scoop of ice cream on each of 4 serving dishes. Spoon the warm berries over the ice cream and serve immediately.

4 SERVINGS

BALLOON BISCUITS

Surprise! The marshmallows tucked inside these dessert biscuits disappear during the baking, leaving a sweet hollow shell. For a wonderful variation, substitute 1-inch chunks of banana for the marshmallows.

4 tablespoons butter
½ cup sugar
¼ teaspoon cinnamon
2 packages (4½ ounces each) refrigerated buttermilk
    biscuits
12 large marshmallows

1. Preheat the oven to 425 degrees F. Line a large baking sheet with a piece of parchment or wax paper or spray with nonstick vegetable coating.

2. Cut the butter into small pieces and place in a glass pie plate. Microwave on High for 30 to 60 seconds, until the butter is melted. In a small bowl, combine the sugar and cinnamon.

3. Remove the biscuits from the package. Roll or pat each one out to a 4-inch circle. Place a marshmallow in the center of a biscuit. Bring the dough up to enclose the marshmallow completely. Pinch the ends to seal.

4. Holding the sealed ends, roll the top and sides of the biscuit in the butter, then in the cinnamon-sugar. Place on the baking sheet, seam side down. Repeat with the remaining ingredients.

5. Bake the biscuits on the middle rack of the oven for 8 to 10 minutes, until golden brown.

12 BISCUITS

CHOCOLATE POTS DE CRÈME

This is so simple and so much better than packaged chocolate pudding, it will become a staple in your dessert repertoire. If you whip this recipe together a few minutes before dinner, it will be ready to serve for dessert.

1⅓ cups half-and-half
  1 cup semisweet chocolate chips
  3 tablespoons sugar
  3 large egg yolks
  1 teaspoon vanilla extract

1. Pour the half-and-half into a 1-quart glass or ceramic bowl and microwave, uncovered, on High for 2½ to 3 minutes, or just until it begins to boil.

2. Place the chocolate chips and sugar in a food processor. Pulse several times to chop the chocolate. Then add the egg yolks and vanilla.

3. With the machine on, slowly add the hot cream through the feed tube. Continue to process for about 30 seconds after the cream has been added, until the mixture is smooth and creamy. Pour into 6-ounce pot de crème cups or ceramic ramekins. Refrigerate for about 30 minutes before serving.

4 SERVINGS

QUICK CHOCOLATE MOUSSE

Although this dessert needs to relax for 20 minutes before it's served, you can put it together in 10, if you're organized. It's delicious served with tart berries.

1 package (6 ounces) semisweet chocolate chips
2 eggs
1 tablespoon coffee liqueur or orange juice
¼ cup sugar
1 cup heavy cream

1. Place the chocolate chips in a 1-quart glass or ceramic bowl. Cover with microwave-safe plastic wrap and place in the microwave. Cook on High for about 2 minutes, just until the chocolate turns shiny, indicating that it has melted.

2. While the chocolate is melting, separate the eggs. In a small bowl, beat the yolks with the coffee liqueur until blended. When the chocolate is melted, stir a few seconds, until smooth. Then beat in the egg yolk mixture.

3. Whip the cream until soft peaks form. Fold the melted chocolate into the whipped cream. Beat the egg whites until stiff but not dry. Gently fold the beaten whites into the chocolate mixture. Pour into serving dishes and refrigerate for about 20 minutes, or until dessert time.

6 SERVINGS

FRUIT CRISP

It took several sweet trials, but we finally figured out how to make fruit crisp in 10 minutes. The choice of fruit is up to you. Pick what is ripest and most appealing. Try using mixed berries, sliced peaches or a combination of peaches and berries.

6 cups cut-up fruit (fresh or frozen)
½ cup sugar
2 cups crushed vanilla wafers
1 cup chopped walnuts (4 ounces)
8 tablespoons (1 stick) butter

1. Place the fruit in a shallow 1½-quart ceramic or tempered glass casserole. Sprinkle the sugar over the fruit and stir to combine. Place the casserole in a microwave oven. Cook on High for 6 minutes, or until the fruit is bubbly, stirring gently after 3 minutes.

2. Preheat the broiler. While the fruit is cooking, combine the cookie crumbs and nuts in a bowl. Stir to mix. Cut the butter into small pieces and add to the crumbs and nuts. Pinch quickly between your fingers to blend.

3. Remove the fruit from the microwave. Sprinkle the nut crumbs evenly over the top and broil 3 to 4 inches from the heat for 2 minutes, or until the crumbs are browned.

6 TO 8 SERVINGS

LEMON CLOUD PIE

Buttery lemon curd is the surprise ingredient in this luscious pie filling. You'll usually find it in the better jams and jellies section of your supermarket. Spoon the fluffy mixture into individual tart shells or into one larger crust. Then arrange fresh strawberries or a combination of your favorite seasonal fruit on top. Your guests will never guess that you only spent 5 minutes making it, if you don't tell them.

1 jar (about 11 ounces) lemon curd
1 cup heavy cream
1 ready-to-serve graham cracker crust (8-inch diameter)
1 pint fresh strawberries

1. Stir the lemon curd until it's smooth. Whip the cream until it doubles in volume and forms soft peaks. Gently stir a large spoonful of the whipped cream into the lemon curd to lighten it. Then fold in the remaining whipped cream. Spoon the lemon filling into the prepared crust.

2. Remove the stems of the strawberries. Rinse and dry them. Cut the strawberries in half and arrange them on top of the lemon filling. Refrigerate until serving time.

6 TO 8 SERVINGS

LINGONBERRY TRIFLE

This traditional British dessert can be assembled quickly if you use a prepared pound cake (we prefer the all-butter kind), a pudding mix and preserved berries.

1 package (3.4 ounces) instant vanilla pudding mix
2 cups milk
1 pound cake (10¾ ounces), preferably all-butter
1 cup jarred lingonberries in sugar
1 cup heavy cream

1. Pour the pudding mix into a medium bowl. Add the milk and stir for about 30 seconds. Let the pudding stand for 3 minutes.

2. Meanwhile, cut the pound cake into ½-inch-thick slices. Line the bottom of a 1½-quart serving bowl, preferably glass, with slices of cake.

3. Spoon half the lingonberries over the cake. Pour all the pudding over the berries.

4. Fit another layer of cake slices over the pudding and top with the remaining berries.

5. Beat the cream until soft peaks form; spoon over the top. Cover and refrigerate the trifle if not serving right away.

6 TO 8 SERVINGS

MOCHA ICE CREAM PIE

With graham cracker and chocolate crumb crusts available
already prepared, and dozens of different flavors of ice cream,
you could create a different frozen pie every night for weeks.

1 pint vanilla ice cream
1 prepared chocolate crumb crust (8 inches in diameter)
1 quart coffee ice cream
1 cup fudge sauce
⅔ cup toasted pecans (optional)

1. Spoon the vanilla ice cream into the bottom of the crumb
crust. Generally ice cream softens enough in the time that it takes
to get home from the supermarket. If it is too hard to work with,
however, just place the carton in the microwave and cook on
High for 3 seconds.

2. Spoon the coffee ice cream over the vanilla. Cover and place
the pie in the freezer if you aren't planning to serve it right away.

3. Just before serving, warm the fudge sauce in the microwave on
High for about 45 seconds to 1 minute, stirring once. Pour the
sauce over the ice cream and sprinkle on the pecans, if you like
them. Cut into wedges and serve.

6 TO 8 SERVINGS

ORANGE ZABAGLIONE

Flavoring a classic zabaglione with orange juice creates a refreshing dessert that's especially nice with fresh blackberries or strawberries. Of course, you can use Marsala or white wine instead.

8 large egg yolks
3 tablespoons sugar
⅔ cup orange juice
1 tablespoon orange zest
1 pint blackberries or strawberries

1. Pour about 2 inches of water into the bottom of a double boiler and bring to a simmer. In the top of the double boiler, whisk together the egg yolks and sugar.

2. Place the top of the double boiler over, but not touching, the simmering water. Slowly whisk in the orange juice and orange zest. Continue cooking and stirring until the mixture is light and creamy, 4 to 6 minutes.

3. Serve the warm zabaglione over the fresh blackberries.

4 SERVINGS

AMARETTO STUFFED PEARS

Microwave expert Suzie Friedenthal convinced us of the virtues of "cooking" in the microwave oven with fast dessert recipes, such as these luscious baked pears. You can also substitute nectarines, peaches or apricots.

2 large pears (ripe but still firm)
4 amaretti or almond macaroons
⅓ cup amaretto (almond-flavored liqueur)
¼ cup chopped pecans
2 teaspoons grated orange zest

1. Rinse and dry the pears. Cut them in half and remove the cores. Scoop out about 2 teaspoons of pear from the center of each half and coarsely chop. Crumble the cookies.

2. In a small bowl, combine the chopped fruit with the cookies, amaretto, pecans and orange zest. Mix until well blended.

3. Fill each pear half with a quarter of the fruit filling. Arrange the pears, filled side up, in a circular pattern in a glass pie plate. Cover them with a sheet of waxed paper. Microwave on High for 4 to 5 minutes, or until the pears are tender. Serve warm.

4 SERVINGS

PEACHES WITH MARZIPAN AND VANILLA RUM CREAM

4 large ripe peaches
½ cup marzipan (almond paste)
1 cup vanilla ice cream
¼ cup rum
1 tablespoon sliced almonds

1. Bring a small pot of water to a boil. Dip the peaches in the water for 30 seconds each, then remove them and rinse under cold water. The skin will slip off easily.

2. Preheat the broiler. Cut the peaches in half and remove the pits. Divide the marzipan into 8 portions, 1 tablespoon each. Shape each piece of marzipan into a small ball. Stuff the peach halves with the marzipan.

3. Place the stuffed peaches on a broiler pan with the marzipan side up. Broil 3 to 4 inches from the heat for 3 minutes, until the peaches are heated through and the marzipan is lightly browned.

4. Place the ice cream in a medium glass or ceramic bowl and microwave on High for 10 seconds, to soften slightly. Beat the ice cream and rum together until blended. Spoon over the peaches and garnish with the sliced almonds.

8 SERVINGS

FRESH PLUM TARTS

Our children got into the spirit and made up this recipe. It was so good we had to include it.

6 fresh plums
2 tablespoons sugar
4 single-serving graham cracker crusts (3 inches in diameter)
¼ cup prepared whipped topping

1. Rinse and dry the plums and cut a slit in the top of each one. Place the plums in a 1-quart glass or ceramic bowl and place in a microwave oven. Microwave on High for 3 minutes.

2. With a teaspoon, remove the plum pits. Sprinkle the sugar over the plums and stir to dissolve.

3. Spoon the warm plums evenly into the 4 crusts. Top each with 1 tablespoon whipped topping and serve immediately.

4 SERVINGS

STRAWBERRY PARFAITS

Pretty as a picture, parfaits are always a treat. If you don't have tall, narrow parfait glasses, use wine goblets or any glass dessert dishes. Feel free to substitute fresh raspberries and blackberries in season for the strawberries, with raspberry or blackberry sherbet.

1 pint fresh strawberries
2 to 3 tablespoons sugar
1 pint vanilla ice cream
½ pint strawberry sherbet
6 amaretti or almond macaroons

1. Rinse, hull and slice the strawberries. Toss them with 2 tablespoons sugar. Taste and add the third tablespoon sugar, if needed.

2. In 6 parfait glasses or other dessert dishes, layer the strawberries alternately with the vanilla ice cream and strawberry sherbet.

3. Crush the cookies and sprinkle them on top of the parfaits. Serve immediately or cover with plastic wrap and place in the freezer until serving time.

6 SERVINGS

INDEX